THE CHRYSANTHEMUM AND THE EAGLE

THE CHRYSANTHEMUM AND THE EAGLE

THE FUTURE OF U.S.–JAPAN RELATIONS

RYUZO SATO

NEW YORK UNIVERSITY PRESS
New York and London

NEW YORK UNIVERSITY PRESS
New York and London

Library of Congress Cataloging-in-Publication Data
Satō, Ryūzō, 1931–
[Kiku to washi. English]
The chrysanthemum and the eagle : the future of U.S.-Japan
relations / Ryūzō Satō.
p.   cm.
Includes bibliographical references and index.
ISBN 0-8147-7971-9 (alk. paper)
1. United States—Relations—Japan. 2. Japan—Relations—United
States. I. Title
E183.8.J3S2413 1994
303.48′273052—dc20   93-33592
CIP

New York University Press books are printed on acid-free paper,
and their binding materials are chosen for strength and durability.

Manufactured in the United States of America

10 9 8 7 6 5 4 3 2 1

CONTENTS

PREFACE

Several years ago when reporters asked Crown Prince Naruhito to describe the qualities he was looking for in a future wife, he replied, "I want to marry someone who has the same sense of values that I have."

Although the concept of values is taken very seriously in both the United States and Europe, it has attracted little public attention in Japan until recently. Even the expression that means "values" in Japanese is not very old. If we think about it, however, frictions are bound to arise in any relationship—be it a marriage or a relationship between two countries—if the two partners have major differences in priorities, in the things that each side considers important in their lives. If partners don't share similar values, they will have to spend enormous amounts of energy reaching an agreement.

When my book *The Chrysanthemum and the Eagle* first came out in Japanese, George Bush was president of the United States. In 1994, Bill Clinton resides in the White House, and Morihisa Hosokawa is Japan's prime minister. Much has been made of the fact that this is the first Democratic administration in twelve years and that Clinton is the youngest president since John Kennedy. But more important than these superficial changes is the change in values they represent. An understanding of these values is likely to be crucial for understanding the personality of the Clinton administration and may also offer insights that will help us predict the future direction of U.S.–Japanese relations.

President Clinton has been described as a rare individual who was elected despite public misgivings about his avoidance of the draft, use of marijuana, and marital infidelity. Considering that twenty or thirty years ago the presidential hopes of men like Adlai Stevenson and Nelson Rockefeller were blighted merely because they were divorced, the criteria for judging the qualities American voters are looking for in their political leaders have clearly undergone a major change. American values have changed with the times.

If the key words of the Clinton administration are "values for a new generation," how will this be reflected in U.S.–Japanese relations? First, this administration will not be bound by ideology or labels, but will be results-oriented. This will mean a tougher policy toward process-oriented Japan—Japan will be told to show results and not try to get by with explanations or excuses. Furthermore, the participation of women in public affairs will be greater than ever. Barbara Bush was famous for being a good wife in the traditional sense of the word, devoted to playing a supportive but clearly subordinate role to her husband. Hillary Rodham Clinton projects the image of the modern career woman with abilities and values of her own, who is capable of carving out a position for herself independent of her husband's status or occupation. In that sense, the fact that career woman Masako Owada will one day become empress may provide the rest of the world with a new insight into Japan—the Japanese sense of values may not be quite so different as some people have tended to believe.

Apart from the much ballyhooed appointments of women and minorities to the cabinet, the new administration has no notable star players. Such a lineup is perhaps suited to the multifaceted operations it will have to undertake. Now that the world has plunged headlong into the post-cold war era, the United States urgently needs to make the shift from a military to a peacetime economy. Yet ethnic conflicts, no longer held in check by the two superpowers, are multiplying. As the flames of ethnic hatreds flare up all over the globe, a number of problems must be dealt with simultaneously. The situation calls for team work rather than for the grandstand plays of such famous former secretaries of state as John Foster Dulles, Robert McNamara, Henry Kissinger, or James Baker.

Although I have used the expression "a change in values" to describe the new administration, that does not mean that everything has changed overnight. Life, liberty, and the pursuit of happiness, the fundamental concepts on which the United States was founded, remain a constant source of American values despite the transfer of power. Still, as I discuss in this book, the weight given to each of these rights changes to reflect the political philosophy—conservative or liberal—of the president in power.

If, for example, the Bush administration could be defined in terms of Hamiltonian elitism, President Clinton's political shading might be called a Jeffersonian populism. This liberal spirit reveals itself in policies that show greater tolerance toward people of color, women, the socially disadvantaged, and homosexuals. Clinton's economic policies, however, have a conservative tinge to them. They are centered on domestic economic concerns and give priority to American companies. A Clinton administration is emerging that is liberal on social issues but conservative as far as economic policy is concerned.

One other aspect of U.S. policy that will continue to affect U.S.–Japanese relations is the view of economic strength as a national security issue, a view that began emerging in the late 1980s and is a central issue in this book. The fact that President Clinton has set up a new cabinet-level National Economic Council on the model of the already-existing National Security Council is a clear sign that he intends to treat economic policy on the same footing as military strategy. Because Clinton believes that America's future depends on a revitalization of the U.S. economy, his administration will approach the issue of strengthening and raising America's international competitiveness as the economic equivalent of war.

In 1990, when the Japanese version of *The Chrysanthemum and the Eagle* first appeared, the Japan-is-different controversy had erupted in the United States, and in Japan voices were shrilly calling for a "Japan That Can Say No." Undoubtedly, one of the underlying causes of this confrontation atmosphere was the sense of superiority that the Japanese had about their economic prosperity. As Japan's technological nationalism was gathering strength, Japanese banks appeared destined to rule the world, and Japanese brokerages were flush with success from a booming stock market.

From my more than thirty years' experience of living in both the United States and Japan, I instinctively felt there was something abnormal about this situation. In the Japanese version of this book I made light of Japanese pride in their country's economic power. I also made the point that Japanese pacifism is not shared by the rest of the world and urged Japan to discuss the role of the Japanese Self-Defense Force instead of treating it as a taboo topic. These problems have subsequently become mainstream issues, and today even the Japanese Socialist party is expounding the need for Japan to make a greater contribution to international society.

I am not a social critic nor am I in the business of predicting the future, yet many of the points I made in my book about U.S.–Japan relations have since come true. This is not because I am an expert on these matters; I have merely written what is obvious to anyone who looks at Japan from the outside. Furthermore, the essence of what I had to say then remains unchanged even now after so many enormous changes have occurred.

In the case of the Gulf War, for instance, the memory of the U.S.-led coalition force's ferocious land and air attack on the Iraqi army is still relatively fresh in most people's minds, yet right up until the bombing began, almost all the so-called military experts who appeared on Japanese television made the absurd assertion that America was unlikely to embark on the use of force. The idealism and pacifism of these Japanese peaceniks were so laughable in international society that—it was said—the only people who were unaware of what was really going on were Saddam Hussein and the Japanese. The United States acted as I always predicted it would, but because most Japanese tend to view the world from the vantage point of their own physical and spiritual insularity, they completely failed to recognize what the rest of the world took for granted. Unfortunately, that still remains true today. Famine in Africa, ethnic strife in the Middle East and Eastern Europe, the perilous process of democratization in Russia—there are storm clouds everywhere one looks. The difference between Japan, which is relatively peaceful and prosperous even in a recession, and the harsh international climate is so enormous that it is hard for most Japanese to comprehend. They would like to close their eyes to the realities of the world outside the Japanese archipelago. Few if any attempts have been made to eliminate what has become the trademark of Japanese behavior in international society—keeping its pocketbook open and its mouth shut.

One of the major differences between Japan and the United States is that America is not allowed the luxury of insularity. As the sole remaining superpower, another topic I deal with in this book, the United States is expected not only to act but also to lead. Although the Clinton administration may have promised to "focus on the economy like a laser," international demands make that a difficult promise to fulfill. On another level, however, Americans tend to be just as insular as the Japanese. Confident of the rightness of their actions, they are often shockingly ignorant of, or indifferent to, the opinions of others.

Americans suffer from an obvious lack of a real understanding of Japan, and the media in the United States do little to help the situation. On February 17, 1991, for example, the *New York Times*'s account of the Japanese government's baby bonus plan began: "With its crowded roads, overstuffed commuter trains and cramped housing, Japan would hardly seem to be in need of more people. So when the government recently started telling the Japanese to bear more children, many people, especially women, became incensed." This is not wrong as far as it goes, but I can't help feeling that the reporter's strong individualism led him to downplay the elementary economic issues involved: the steady decline in Japan's population, the over-concentration of people in large cities accompanied by depopulation of rural areas, and the prospect that by the year 2025 one in every four Japanese will be over the age of sixty-five. Keeping the birthrate low may be crucial for India and the People's Republic of China, but it can do more harm than good in Japan.

Having observed firsthand how little people overseas know about what is going on in Japan, I feel strongly about increasing the channels through which information about Japan is transmitted to the rest of the world. The Japanese must make themselves better understood. Information overflows within Japan, which rightly prides itself as being in the vanguard of the Information Age, yet a great deal of the most important news never even gets translated, let alone disseminated through international media.

On the other hand, despite the prominence the Japanese media give to American affairs, the Japanese people are surprisingly ignorant about the United States. Information about America in the Japanese press or on Japanese television tends to be very superficial, a repetition of received ideas with no effort to look behind the platitudes. When I started writing the Japanese version of this book back in 1989, criticisms of Japan in the United States were growing more and more shrill. Japan-bashing on one side of the Pacific had given rise to America-bashing on the other. During this period of trans-Pacific bad feeling, I tried to draw on my own experience of life in America to go beyond the stereotypes perpetuated in the Japanese media and look at some of the basic divergences in the two countries' priorities, in what I referred to earlier as their sense of values. I firmly believe no true solution to the frictions that have exacerbated U.S.–Japanese relations can be achieved without first delving into these problems and tracing them back to their origins.

Much has happened in the world since the Japanese version of this book first appeared. The Japanese economy, which had been held up as an example to the world during the 1980s, was a bubble that eventually burst. Meanwhile, outside Japan, a number of major changes have occurred in quick succession: the collapse of Soviet communism and the disintegration of the Soviet Union; the Gulf War; the end to the myth of a never-ending rise in Japanese land prices; a global economic slowdown; the first Japanese soldiers to be sent abroad since World War II; the break-up of the largest faction of the LDP and formation of a coalition government in Japan; the end of twelve years of Republican administrations in the United States—these and other events have profoundly altered the political and economic landscape. Though tensions between the

United States and Japan do not seem quite as acute as they were in 1989 when I was writing the Japanese version of this book, mutual ignorance and misunderstanding still prevail in U.S.–Japanese relationships. Today advances in transportation and communications technology have just about perfected the physical links between the United States and Japan. In rewriting and updating my book for an American audience, I hope to contribute in my own small way to bridging the communications gap between our two countries.

Many people have worked behind the scenes to make this book possible. On the Japanese side, I would like to thank Ms. Sawako Noma, president of Kodansha, which published the original Japanese version of this book, and Kodansha editors Tadashi Ichikawa, Takashi Ogose, and Sueo Muraoka. My deep gratitude also goes to Tsuneo Watanabe, president of the Yomiuri Shimbun Company, which awarded the Japanese version of this book the First Yomiuri Rondansho Prize for writings in the social sciences; to Ichiro Kato, the chairman of the selection committee, whose valuable comments prompted me to write a sequel; and to then Prime Minister Toshiki Kaifu, who did me the honor of speaking at the award ceremony.

On this side of the Pacific, my special thanks go to translator Jean Hoff for all her efforts. At the Center for Japan–U.S. Business and Economic Studies, Hiroki Nikaido and Laurie Jaeger helped track down stray details, and my associate director Rama Ramachandran and the Center coordinator Myra Engel read over the final version and made many helpful suggestions. I would also like to express my appreciation to Colin Jones, director of the New York University Press, whose comments were extremely useful in clarifying issues for an American readership. I take this occasion to extend to all of them my sincere thanks.

THE CHRYSANTHEMUM AND THE EAGLE

ONE

THE RISE
OF REVISIONISM

The "Hawks" and
the "Chrysanthemum Club"

A New Containment Policy? Early in 1991, I had a discussion with James Fallows, the Washington editor of the *Atlantic Monthly,* who is calling for drastic changes in U.S. policy toward Japan. During the course of our conversation he made a remark that helps explain the mixed feelings Americans have toward Japan. When General Douglas MacArthur returned to the United States after heading the Allied occupation of Japan, Fallows said, the general was certain he had made Japan into an American clone, a notion that was apparently shared by most Americans in those days. In the course of subsequent Japan–U.S. negotiations, however, it soon became clear that, far from having been re-created in America's image, Japan had emerged as a country poles apart from the United States. The illusion and its betrayal, Fallows pointed out, underlie the

1

frustrations of the American people in their dealings with Japan.

Still, just as no two people look exactly alike, no two countries are the same. Each country has its own culture and traditions. Even the occupation authorities knew that; all they hoped to redesign in the American image were Japan's political institutions and economic systems. The drastic reforms they launched—land reform, dissolution of the *zaibatsu* (big financial and industrial combines) and the old class system, women's suffrage, equal opportunity in education, and freedom to unionize—did indeed make Japan totally different from what it had been before the war. Today, a half century after Pearl Harbor, the democratic political system and the capitalist economic system the United States implanted on Japanese soil have been thoroughly acculturated and indigenized, rendering them completely different from their parent models. It is easy to understand why some Americans stress the need to drastically revise a Japan policy that was adopted by the United States at a time when it thought it was dealing with a country which had the same systems as its own.

I first came to the United States in the late 1950s as a Fulbright exchange student, and for more than thirty years I have spent part of each year in the United States and part in Japan. During that time I have watched American attitudes toward Japan and Japanese products undergo a profound change. When I was a student in Baltimore I remember going to look for a second-hand car. "What about that Japanese car over there?" I asked. The salesman, a big man about six foot three or four, put his foot on the bumper and shook the car back and forth. "You don't want to buy this," he said. "This isn't a car; it's a Japanese toy."

No one talks about Japanese toys today. Although the atmosphere of fear and hostility has eased somewhat as the United States and Japan have both turned inward to deal with their respective domestic economic problems, many Americans have come to regard Japan's economic success as a threat to their own way of life. Sensationalist accounts that imply Japan is out to dominate the world economically—although it has no such intention—merely increase Americans' unease during a period in which the U.S. economy is being radically restructured.

Since World War II, the enemy, both militarily and ideologically, has been the Soviet Union. But the 1980s saw an extraordinary reversal in American feelings toward what President Ronald Reagan at the beginning of his term of office had called "the evil empire." By the end of the decade Mikhail Gorbachev's *perestroika* policy had led to a new detente, brought an end to the cold war, and ushered in a new era of East-West cooperation. Since then, the Communist party has been ousted from power in all the countries of the former Soviet bloc, including the Soviet Union itself. By the end of 1991, the Union of Soviet Socialist Republics had ceased to exist, and Russia and its former allies have begun experimenting with a free-market economy. Capitalism has triumphed over communism, and the policy of Soviet containment first articulated by George Kennan has been an overwhelming success.

In 1947 an article entitled "The Sources of Soviet

Conduct" by Mr. X (later identified as George Kennan) appeared in the U.S. journal *Foreign Affairs.* The United States, Kennan wrote:

> must continue to regard the Soviet Union as a rival, not a partner, in the political arena.... Russia, as opposed to the western world in general, is still by far the weaker party.... Soviet power ... bears within it the seeds of its own decay. ... Soviet society may well contain deficiencies which will eventually weaken its own total potential. This would of itself warrant the United States entering with reasonable confidence upon a policy of firm containment.

History has corroborated the truth of these views, written more than forty-five years ago. America's "Russian containment policy" has proven to be a successful strategy against the Soviet Union.

What if, in the above quote, "Japan" were substituted for the "Soviet Union," and "in the economic arena" for "in the political arena"? This may not have been what James Fallows had in mind when he wrote his article "Containing Japan" for the *Atlantic Monthly* in 1989, but such a statement would perfectly encapsulate a Japanese containment policy. If America regards Japan as an economic adversary, and if, as some maintain, concepts of democracy, capitalism, and a free economy and society are different in Japan from what they are in the Western world, then "containing Japan" would be strongly persuasive as an effective policy measure.

Implicit in America's view of itself is the belief that the United States has the strongest military power, the richest economy, and the most desirable ideological system in the world. The collapse of communism has provided stunning corroboration for the first and third of these premises. But is America in fact the world's richest country? How can one account for the fact that at the same time communism was in retreat in Eastern Europe, vast sums of "Japan money" were buying up America and that one U.S. institution after another passed into Japanese hands, including—to the great indignation of the American people—such American icons as Rockefeller Center and Columbia Pictures, which the October 9, 1989, issue of *Newsweek* called "a piece of America's soul"? Or to put the question another way, why does America, the most powerful country in the world, with the most abundant resources and the most stable and desirable political system, suffer from twin budget and current account deficits, and why has it become the world's largest debtor nation?

Clearly, Japan must be "unfair." That is the easiest line of reasoning for the American public to understand. And, in fact, when one starts to reexamine Japan from this premise, a number of illogical or unfair practices begin to emerge—protection, controls, bid rigging, corporate groupings, winning bids of a single yen, insider trading, and disregard for the consumer. Such practices fueled the criticisms of a new school of thinking about Japan—revisionism—which began to make its presence felt in the United States at the end of the 1980s.

The views of the revisionists can be summed up as follows: For a long time America has believed that Japan is a country which has the same values as itself. That, however, is only an illusion. As the Japanese themselves assert, Japan really is unique. The American concept of free trade does not hold true for the Japanese, and the various attempts to get Japan to change have been fundamentally mistaken. From now on America should shift policies and adopt radically different measures to deal with this very different country. The effect of these arguments has been to elevate Japan to the status of an ideological opponent of the United States.

The Hawks, the Apologists, and the Japanologists. The *Newsweek* article described the two schools of thought on "the Japan problem" as a debate between the hawks and "the Chrysanthemum Club" and identified the leading members on both sides. The trade hawks, pejoratively referred to as "Japan bashers," advocate that the United States adopt a tougher stand on trade and economic issues. In addition to Fallows, they include Richard Gephardt, the Democratic whip in the House of Representatives; John Danforth, the Republican senator from Missouri; Clyde Prestowitz, a former trade negotiator with the Commerce Department and the author of the book *Trading Places;* Karel van Wolferen, a Dutch journalist who wrote *The Enigma of Japanese Power*; and Chalmers Johnson, a professor at the University of California at San Diego who wrote *MITI and the Japanese Miracle.*

What most of these men have in common is that they are hard-liners who know Japan well. Their criticisms are based on a thorough knowledge of Japanese history and Japanese institutions. Clyde Prestowitz, for example, as an official in the Department of Commerce, had direct experience in dealing with the Japanese Ministry of International Trade and Industry (MITI). Karel van Wolferen and James Fallows have both lived in Japan. Their experience lends substance to their criticisms and gives their observations greater validity. Naturally, this has had a strong impact on the American people.

The traditionalists who espouse orthodox views on the importance of the U.S.–Japan strategic alliance and the value of a free-trade economy have been called "the Chrysanthemum Club" or labeled "apologists" for Japan because they defend the Japanese position. Former ambassador to Japan Mike Mansfield is a prime example. During his tenure as ambassador, Mansfield insisted that the United States and Japan have "the most important bilateral relationship in the world, bar none" and maintained that the chief problem between the two countries was the U.S. budget deficit. James Baker, Richard Cheney, Richard Darman, and Michael Boskin were members of the Bush administration who believe that little is to be gained by being overly critical of Japan. Others named in the *Newsweek* article as members of the Chrysanthemum Club include Ezra Vogel, author of *Japan as Number One*; Professor James Ableggen of Sophia University in Tokyo; lobbyist Stanton Anderson; and Elliot Richardson, attorney general during the Nixon administration.

These two groups, for good or ill, have the greatest influence on policy- and opinion-making in the United States today. But in addition to the hawks and the Chrysanthemum Club, there is in fact a third group in America who are fluent in Japanese, have a profound knowledge of Japanese history and culture, and are regarded as having a sympathetic understanding of Japan. Perhaps the best known of these scholars and researchers would be the late Edwin Reischauer, the former ambassador to Japan, who wrote:

Certainly much of what the revisionists have pointed out is true. But they take a short-term view of Japan. When they claim that Japan does not change, they are speaking about the period after the Second World War. If one looks at Tokugawa Japan [1600–1868] or Meiji Japan [1868–1912] or Showa Japan [1926–1989], one can see that Japan has changed radically. I believe Japan is a country of enormous flexibility and resilience; as the times change, it will inevitably change as well and will be able to avoid even seemingly unavoidable frictions. In this respect the assertions of the revisionists are mistaken.

Although these comments, which I have translated from an article in Japanese by Professor Reischauer in the February 28, 1989, *Asahi Shimbun,* are certainly pro-Japanese, not all Japanologists should be thought of as members of the Chrysanthemum Club.

Japanologists are first and foremost scholars and not mainstream American policymakers. Until recently they have tended to be individuals with a personal interest in Japan, those who were born there perhaps or who lived there in their childhood. Because they do not represent ordinary American interests, they may lecture about Japan or show their understanding of matters Japanese or participate in seminars on Japanese subjects, but with a few notable exceptions—Reischauer himself being one of them—they are in no position to exert any influence on actual government policy-making.

Herein lies the major difference between Japanologists and the members of the Chrysanthemum Club. Whether or not the latter can speak Japanese or have any deep understanding of Japan, they are mainstream politicians or political advisers who can affect the U.S. government's Japan policy. People like Michael Boskin and Richard Darman know almost nothing about Japan. But others like Mike Mansfield have a thorough knowledge of the country. What these people have in common is that they are part of the American political mainstream and understand its logic. The pro-Japan argument boils down to this: U.S.–Japan relations are based on mutual advantage, so disputes must be resolved in an objective and realistic fashion. Nothing productive can come of Japan-bashing. Bashing on the one side merely invites bashing on the other, and each country ends up hurting its own cause.

Under the Bush administration, the Chrysanthemum Club was in the ascendancy; the Clinton administration is more hawkish toward Japan. The current head of the Council of Economic Advisers, Laura Tyson, is widely considered to be a hawk. As mentioned earlier, many of the hawks are experts on Japan. Most of them have had "Japanese experience" and are the very people one might expect to be sympathetic to Japan because they understand the potential harm that will result if U.S.–Japan relations deteriorate any further. That makes their arguments all the more convincing to the American public, who feel that "if people who have lived in Japan say so, then Japan really must be different." That they have become outspokenly critical is a tragedy for Japan.

The Conflict between Feelings and Logic. Members of the Chrysanthemum Club come to Japan's defense out of a sense of rational self-interest. The hawks' view of Japan, on the other hand, is both more emotional and more deeply grounded in experience because it is derived from what they have actually encountered firsthand. This basis in fact, not theory, has helped to strengthen the persuasiveness of their arguments. Japan, too, has a number of America specialists who regularly air their views about the United States, but few of these self-styled experts have actually had the experience of living in the United States with their families for several years. The arguments of Japanese who have no firsthand knowledge of America inevitably seem abstract and superficial and carry as little conviction as the claims that some Japanese commentators with no particular expertise in engineering or technology have made about Japan's status as a technological superpower. As Professor Fumio Shimura of North Carolina State University noted in the February 1992 issue of *This Is Yomiuri*, Japanese mass-produced computer chips may be the best in the world, but like nails in the construction of a building, they are not of much use by themselves.

In America today the quarrel between the hawks and the Chrysanthemum Club has evolved into a head-on collision between two groups in the political mainstream responsible for formulating U.S. policy. U.S.–Japan relations have gone far beyond the stage when those who knew something about Japan clashed with those who did not. This fact has extremely serious implications for understanding the true nature of Japan–U.S. frictions. As Japan has emerged as a major world economic power, Japan–U.S. relations have come to be included among America's main policy concerns. For that very reason, a single misstep in policy on the part of either Japan or the United States could have dire consequences.

From a different perspective, the quarrel between

the hawks and the Chrysanthemum Club might be regarded as a conflict between emotional and logical arguments. Against the more emotional hawks, the Chrysanthemum Club resorts to logic to make its point. Which, then, will prevail—feelings or logic? Reason teaches that logic should win, but emotional arguments have often carried the day, and sometimes in the long run the choices based on them have worked out for the best. What, for example, was the rationale behind the Japanese automobile industry thirty or forty years ago when it was still in its infancy? For a small country, with roads little better than farm tracks, an attempt to promote an auto industry flew in the face of reason. That was the logic of the economists of the time, not to mention the Ministry of International Trade and Industry (MITI). But the people making cars felt differently. No matter how farfetched their plans seemed to others, they had faith that they could make the Japanese automotive industry the best in the world. Today, it is clear their faith was justified.

Economic logic, in other words, does not always produce the right results. In relations between countries, especially, emotional arguments often get the better of reason. In the conflict between the hawks and the Chrysanthemum Club, it cannot be assumed that rational arguments will win. Ninety-nine percent of the American people have never been to Japan and know nothing about the realities of life there. Logic is based upon knowledge, and emotional arguments thrive on ignorance. As the hawks' propaganda penetrates grassroots America and emotional arguments dictate public opinion, the logic of a free-market economy is being overwhelmed by the Japan-is-different argument.

Is Japan Really Different?

Containing Japan. Just as many Americans overreacted to what they perceived as America-bashing in the pirated English version of *The Japan That Can Say "No"* by Akio Morita and Shintaro Ishihara (see chapter 2), many Japanese have overreacted to James Fallows's article "Containing Japan," which they regard as Japan-bashing. This trans-Pacific exchange of bad feelings seems to have been provoked by the titles of these two works rather than by their actual contents.

In English the nuances of the word *contain* are not nearly as strong as they are for the Japanese word *fūjikome,* which was used in the translation of Fallows's article. *Fūjikome* has strong overtones—it would be used, for example, in describing the sealing off of a nuclear reactor where an accident has occurred. As a translation for the English word *contain,* it is a bit too strong. The meaning of *contain* is essentially defensive; the overtones of the word *fūjikome* are a hundred-percent offensive and imply a preemptive strike.

In one sense, America has already tried "containing Japan." To counter the flood of Japanese imports in areas like textiles, steel, consumer electronics, and automobiles, it launched a containment policy that forced Japan to accept export controls and voluntary restraints. To counter a soaring trade deficit, it embarked on a containment policy that put pressure on Japan to open its markets and increase domestic demand. The 1985 Plaza Accord was yet another attempt at a containment policy. To redress the trade imbalance, the finance ministers of the five major industrialized countries (the United States, Japan, West Germany, Great Britain, and France) agreed to a currency realignment at a meeting held in September 1985 at the Plaza Hotel in New York. Despite a drastic downward revaluation, from 240 yen to 120 yen to the dollar between 1985 and 1988, the U.S. balance of trade with Japan improved a mere 15 percent, and Japan continues to maintain a healthy surplus.

Theoretically, if the value of the dollar decreases by half, prices of American goods destined for Japanese markets should also be halved, generating brisk sales that should lead to an increase in U.S. exports and a reduction in the trade deficit. Prices for Japanese goods, on the other hand, should double, causing a slowdown in sales. The resulting decline in Japanese exports should bring about a decline in Japan's trade surplus. That, at least, is what the laws of economics dictate. And, in fact, this occurred in Europe, where a lower dollar led to an American-European trade balance. It did not happen in Japan, however. Foreign goods in Japan remained as expensive as ever, and Japanese goods sold abroad did not double in price. The annual trade deficit with Japan remained—and still remains—around $50 billion. Why? The answer must be that Japan is "different," that structural differences are at work there that do not respond to economic laws.

This is the background against which the revisionists emerged with their call for a reexamination of U.S. premises about Japan. This is what set the stage in 1989 for the most recent round of U.S.–Japan trade negotiations, the Structural Impediments Initiative talks, which were haunted by the threat that Congress would invoke the Super 301 provision of the 1988 Trade Act and impose economic sanctions on Japan and other countries that engage in "unfair" trading practices. In this dangerous atmosphere the use of the word *fūjikome* in the title of the translation of "Containing Japan" was irresponsible. It evoked associations with the ABCD encirclement and the international isolation of Japan on the eve of World War II; it also angered and alarmed the Japanese people and stirred up nationalistic sentiments. No one could have been more surprised by this reaction than the article's author, James Fallows himself.

The Mass Media in the United States and Japan. In November 1989 I had a discussion with James Fallows at the request of a Japanese magazine and television station. Before our talk began, he was very wary of me. His extreme mistrust of the Japanese media seemed quite understandable. The Japanese translation of his article had caused a furor far beyond his wildest expectations, and the Japanese media en masse had made him out to be an enemy of Japan. As he put it, somehow or other, he had become public enemy number one. As an example of the misrepresentations the media had indulged in, Fallows told me the following story.

Fallows had been asked by a television station to discuss his views on the Yellow Peril theory. In the course of that interview, he made the statement that he did not endorse the view that racial prejudice lay at the heart of current American criticisms of Japan. Regrettably, racism did exist in America, but he personally was firmly opposed to those who resorted to this sort of argument, as were America's leading policymakers. He had accepted the television station's invitation, he told me, because he thought it provided a good opportunity to convey the convictions of Americans like himself who regard racial prejudice as something to be ashamed of, and he talked animatedly for several minutes on the subject. Sometime later he heard from the television station that his comments had been cut because they did not fit in with its plans. To learn what these plans had been, he later watched the program with considerable interest. To Fallows's dismay, he discovered the program was not about whether the Yellow Peril theory was valid. It took American racism for granted, and so quite naturally his comments did not fit in.

The program dramatically traced historical events such as the extermination of the aboriginal peoples of Central and South America by the Spanish and the mass slaughter of Native Americans in North America by later white settlers. Stressing the whites' oppression of nonwhites, and relying on the tricks and special effects of television, it conveyed the message that recent American criticisms of Japan are an extension of white America's historical racial prejudices. Where was the conscience of the Japanese mass media, Fallows asked. This program was inflammatory, an abuse of the power of television. Fallows was profoundly incensed.

I too am well aware of the propensity of the Japanese media to sensationalize, and for that reason I resist making comments about U.S.–Japan relations that might lend themselves to overdramatization. Extreme statements, even those made by people who know nothing of America, are prized by the Japanese media because they are easy to report. But the American media are just as bad. When Sony bought Columbia Pictures, *Newsweek* described it as "a piece of America's soul." Columbia had been a nearly bankrupt company nobody seemed much interested in until it was sold to the Japanese. The media then reported its purchase as if Sony had stolen the crown jewels. The same was true with the sale of Rockefeller Center. The media carried on as if the traditional Christmas tree were going to be replaced with a bonsai. When Konishiki, a Hawaiian, won a sumo tournament in November 1989, how did the *New York Times* caption its account of the victory? "An American Is Enthroned and Japan Is Shaken." What nonsense! Far from being shaken, many Japanese were thrilled at Konishiki's success.

In both the United States and Japan such media distortions are everyday occurrences. Driven only by profit-making and rapidly becoming morally bankrupt, the media constantly sensationalize.

After the Berlin Wall, the Japanese Wall. James Fallows has argued that allowing Japan to expand indiscriminately and destructively is not in the best interest of Japan or the rest of the world. I agree with him. Whether these views are correct logically speaking, I cannot say, but I believe that now is not the time to think purely in terms of logic. Speaking from the logic of economics, certainly no one can claim that Japan is wrong. Working without a moment's leisure, saving for the future, caring more about conservation than consumption, offering the world better products at cheaper prices, making money—these are all actions that live up to capitalist ideals.

Capitalism means competition; its dominant principle is that whoever wins, survives. That is the premise upon which neoclassical economic theory is based, and as a modern economist who belongs to this school, I find Japan's actions both logical and correct. But what happens if we advance that argument one step further? If a highly competitive Japan should continue to be as successful as it has been in offering its goods to the world, naturally its profits will increase. As a result, the yen will rise in value and the dollar and all the other currencies in the world will fall. If Japan one-sidedly grows so strong that it tramples on the livelihood of people in other countries, then no matter how many good products it makes, it will gradually become unable to sell them.

Economic textbooks teach that a system of checks and balances, sometimes referred to as the "invisible hand," will operate to check Japan's export strength; there is no need, therefore, for governments to set up safety nets such as tariffs and controls. Viewed from that vantage point, Japan's behavior is quite rational and it is Japan-bashing that is unfair. But is reality adhering to textbook theory? Are these checks and balances operating between America and Japan? Did sales of Japanese goods decline when the value of the yen went up? Was the Japanese surplus erased and a trade balance achieved? After the dollar became cheaper, was the United States able to rapidly expand its exports to Japan?

Unfortunately, events have not transpired the way the textbooks say they should. The system of checks and balances that operates between the United States and Europe does not work between the United States and Japan. Why not? The answer seems to be, as Fallows says, that the customs and institutions within Japan—as seen from the American side—are "different." Consequently, insofar as Western logic does not work in Japan, America must come up with some sort of national policy to take the place of the "invisible hand" in the form either of protectionism or of managed trade. This is what Fallows really means when he speaks of "containing Japan."

The most recent (1989–90) round of bilateral trade negotiations, the U.S.–Japan Structural Impediments Initiative, took place against this background. The SII talks were based on the premise that an underlying factor in the trade imbalance between the United States and Japan was "structural differences"—fundamental divergences in the two countries' economic and social structures. In an effort to ensure more transparent trade practices and a more open marketplace, American negotiators came to the bargaining table armed with a list of nontariff trade barriers that they claimed prevented U.S. access to the Japanese market. Indeed, many practices that the Japanese take for granted seem strange when looked at from outside and certainly do not conform with international rules. Contractors who meet together to decide which of them will get a certain job or companies that submit a bid of one yen in order to win a contract that will result in a long-term relationship and a virtual future monopoly—sleazy bidding practices such as these are carried out as a matter of course not by gangster-controlled syndicates but by top-ranking computer firms and the construction industry. Such practices would be inconceivable in other countries. Bringing them out into the open is highly embarrassing, but they must be exposed so that Japan can prepare for the future.

The Structural Impediments Initiative talks concluded with both sides promising major structural changes. Japanese concessions included promises to curb tax benefits for farmland owners in urban areas, to remove the right of small-store owners to veto the opening of large retail outlets in their neighborhoods, and to increase staff on the Japanese Fair Trade Commission. In return, the United States promised to cut the budget, increase federal support for research and development, strengthen export promotion, and require the adoption of the metric system for federal procurements beginning in 1993. Although the Japanese felt that U.S. interference in Japan's domestic problems was unwarranted, they have more effectively addressed the compromises reached during the talks, whereas until recently under the Clinton administration the United States made no effort at all to comply with Japan's demands to increase savings and decrease the government's budget deficit. Although I do not believe the Structural Impediments Initiative talks produced any significant results, they have somewhat alleviated the tension between the two countries. If they have had the secondary effect of helping to bring Japanese rules in line with international rules, then they were valuable.

By adopting exactly the same policy toward Japan that it has toward its European trading partners, America has incurred a huge trade deficit and run up against an invisible wall that surrounds the Japanese archipelago. Under the circumstances it is not at all strange that Americans have concluded that there is something different about Japan and have decided to rethink their views. Reacting against this new U.S. position, some in Japan have argued that it is America that is different. Certainly, America would appear different from the Japanese perspective; this sort of nationalistic sentiment is quite understandable. But that does not mean Japan can force its rules on the rest of the world. And to believe that America ought to be the one to change is not only impractical but irresponsible. It is unreasonable to expect Americans to understand—let alone put into practice—such Japanese concepts as group solidarity or corporate groupings or to expect them to behave like the employees of Mitsubishi who will drink only Kirin beer. For better or for worse, the postwar world plays by America's rules. That comes with the territory of world leadership, a subject I will discuss in more detail later.

America can manage quite well economically without Japan, but Japan cannot get along without the United States. Some Japanese commentators seem to be unaware that Japan does not exist independently of the rest of the world. They have projected a rosy-colored future for Japan and predict that the twenty-first century will be "the Japanese century," but even if such prospects exist at the microeconomic level, I have my doubts about these optimistic scenarios. Since 1989, Japan's attention has turned in on itself. That year many of Japan's political elite were implicated in the Recruit shares-for-favors scandal and Prime Minister Noboru Takeshita was forced to resign. Voter wrath over the imposition of a 3 percent consumption tax led to the poor showing of the ruling Liberal Democratic party in the Upper House election that July and brought about the ouster of Takeshita's successor, Sosuke Uno, who had been discredited by a sex scandal. While Japan was absorbed by the spectacle of three prime ministers succeeding each other within the space of a single year, the rest of the world greatly changed. The democratic movements in Eastern Europe, the collapse of the Soviet Union, and more recently the U.S.-led victory in the Gulf War after Iraq's invasion of Kuwait have all been taken as proof of the correctness of U.S. foreign policy. As Eastern Europe and the former Soviet Union move toward a free-market economy, the world seems to be revolving around the American axis. Under the circumstances, it should come as no surprise that Americans have shifted their focus to the economic arena and that after the Berlin Wall the next barrier they hope will fall will be the one surrounding Japan.

Does Money Give Anyone the Right to Buy Someone Else's Soul? Economic activities and trends inevitably have their own rules. Economics is the science of finding those rules. The problem is that sometimes an economy operates according to the rules and sometimes it does not. When the latter happens, measures must be taken to counteract events or trends that run counter to expectations.

In the late 1980s Japan was busily buying up American assets with the excess cash from its huge trade surplus. Logically speaking, this activity was a natural consequence wholly in line with the laws of economics. The question is: Should something be allowed to happen just because it accords with economic laws? Shouldn't some consideration be given to whether the activity is ultimately in the best interests of the parties involved? Viewed in that light, the situation takes on a completely different complexion. This is what makes the laws of economics so much more unpredictable than the laws of physics or chemistry. The field of economics has recently come to make greater use of mathematical models and is becoming a more scientific discipline. In North America and Europe it is now regarded as having more in common with the sciences than with the humanities. Because economics deals with people and its testing ground is society rather than a laboratory, however, we should not insist that it is an exact science. Economic problems have a nasty tendency to develop into political and social problems.

When rain falls on a mountain, for example, and forms into a river, it waters the fields at the foot of the mountain and enriches the lives of the people who live there. This is referred to as the workings of nature. But if several inches of rain were to fall in the course of an hour, the river would overflow and the village at the foot of the mountain would be washed away. That, too, is a law of nature, but the villagers do not just sit back and allow this to happen. They build a dam upstream to control a possible flood. And this human action to reverse the laws of nature is praised as a good policy.

Let's transpose this analogy to the economy. Since the end of the 1980s, $50 or $60 billion worth of Japanese investment a year, the equivalent of Japan's annual trade surplus, has flooded through the world, much of it buying up American land, buildings, companies, and even people (lobbyists). Should Americans stand idly by simply because an economic law is operating? Isn't it necessary to build some sort of dam?

When a policy runs counter to economic laws, however, far from being praised—as in the case of flood control—it is criticized as protectionism, regulation, or interference. Why? One reason is that natural phenomena can be readily observed, but economic phenomena are not easy to visualize. We can see the flow of water, but we cannot actually see the flow of investment around the globe. This is puzzling for economists and even more puzzling for ordinary people. But when the flow of investment does become visible, shouldn't policymakers take bold steps, such as containment, even though that means temporarily acting contrary to economic laws?

In the late 1980s Japan's "buying America" became clearly visible to the naked eye. There seemed no end to the land or the companies the Japanese acquired. Japan has argued that it is not the only country to have bought American property, that British holdings are even larger than Japan's. But this argument inadvertently lets the cat out of the bag. The truth is that Japanese investment is rapidly catching up with the British, Dutch, and German investments that have been made over a long period of years. It has been a veritable torrent rather than a gently falling rain, and no one can claim that a torrential rainfall in the space of a few hours has the same effect as an equivalent amount of rain falling over a ten-day period.

This situation is most dramatically manifested in the growth of Japanese direct investment abroad. Valued at a mere $10.6 billion during the period 1975–79, direct investment for 1985–89 had risen to $118.8 billion, a more than tenfold increase in just ten years' time. In the United States alone, Japanese direct investment

went from $67.3 billion in 1989 to $83.5 billion in 1990.*
Thus, more than half of these acquisitions were in the
United States and quite visibly concentrated in Hawaii,
California, and New York. This was not just a torrent
but more like a flash flood.

The analogy can be taken only so far, however. In
the natural world, no one benefits from a flood, but in
the economic world, this flow of investment clearly
was to the benefit of Japan, and inevitably it inflamed
American chauvinism. Excessive growth, excessive
gains in any area, are bound to produce a hostile reaction. According to an opinion poll of American chief
executive officers conducted jointly by the *Nihon Keizai
Shimbun* and the U.S. polling organization Booz Allen
for the *Wall Street Journal,* only 54.8 percent welcomed
Japanese investment in the United States. To give some
idea of how low that figure is, the highest approval rate
for investment by another country was 93.8 percent for
Canada, with Britain, the Netherlands, and Germany
falling between 76.8 and 87.7 percent. The number of
respondents who said Japanese investment was not
welcome was 22.6 percent.

Another reason why this concentrated investment in
the United States was not welcome is that, despite the
strong yen and the weak dollar, America's trade deficit
with Japan has not been reduced at all. The proposal
by Fallows and other revisionists to adopt managed
trade as a containment policy is a reflection of American irritation with this situation. The fact that the

*The slowdown in the Japanese economy has temporarily halted
the growth of Japanese investment abroad, but as Japan's trade
surplus continues to grow, the excess will have to be invested
somewhere, this time most likely in Asia.

United States, the standard bearer for free trade since World War II, has been tempted to adopt a managed trade policy gives some indication of the extent of American frustration. The very term *managed trade* creates a negative impression. It describes a human activity that interferes with the free working of the "invisible hand"—the golden rule of capitalism. The unspoken assumption behind the U.S.–Japan Structural Impediments Initiative talks was that America would desperately like to avoid resorting to such a course.

This is what happens when economic activity does not operate according to logic. Certainly, as Akio Morita, the chairman of Sony, has said, it is not the concentrated outpouring of Japanese exports, but the concentrated American absorption of these products, that is the problem. There is a certain logic, too, in his statement that if Columbia Pictures is a piece of America's soul, then the problem lies not with those who bought it, but with those who were willing to sell it. In economics, however, some ideas cannot be put across simply by brandishing the correct argument, particularly when national pride is linked to economic interests.

America's Sun Has Not Yet Set

The Supremacy of the Dollar. Structural Impediments Initiative talks or "containing Japan"—call it what you will—both are indicative of a desperate fight for the preeminence of the U.S. economy. Why has America, a country whose overwhelming postwar power and affluence led it to assume the roles of the world's banker and policeman, seen its formidable lead in world economic affairs slowly slip away? The answer is inherent in the very nature of the postwar monetary system, the International Monetary Fund (IMF), which was advantageous to the United States in the short run, but not in the long run.

Because the American dollar is the key global currency, other countries have to export to earn foreign currency (dollars) and then use those dollars to buy (import) the things they need. After the war, for example, Japan wanted to import because it had no natural resources, but it needed dollars to do so. It launched an export drive to earn those dollars and, finally, at the end of the 1970s, around the time of the second oil crisis, it achieved a balance between imports and exports. Or, to put it another way, enough profits on sales had built up in the country's coffers so that it could buy whatever it wanted.

On the other hand, because the dollar has been the key currency used by the free world throughout the postwar period and is accepted both at home and abroad, America alone can import whatever it wants without having to export first. With some exaggeration one might even say that as long as the United States prints dollars, it has the right to buy anything in the world. Even without the money readily at hand it can buy on credit. That is one of the advantages of controlling the key currency.

This situation will continue as long as America maintains its grip on world leadership. But when, as now, American competitiveness is declining, controlling the key currency becomes a disadvantage. What was beneficial in the short run becomes a handicap over the long run. The flip side to the short-term advantage of being able to buy anything you want without making any export effort is that two big bills eventually come due—a long-term deterioration of international competitiveness and an ingrained habit of import consumption.

Thus, lurking in the background of the debate about containing Japan are these systemic factors of short-term advantages and long-term disadvantages. This raises the question of whether it might be a good idea to change the system, but in point of fact there is no currency at present that is capable of replacing the dollar as the key currency. And even if there were, the United States would not accept such a course of action. Suppose, for example, that the yen grew even stronger and Japan invested huge sums of money in the IMF, thus eclipsing the U.S. contribution and winning a stronger say for itself. America would be upset. Even if the United States has declined in real strength, it is not likely to give up its prerogatives of world leadership. That is not the way superpowers behave.

If some worldwide upheaval or major cataclysm occurred, the situation would be different. The dollar replaced the pound as the key currency when world leadership shifted from Britain to the United States after two world wars. For leadership to be transferred during peacetime as the result of deliberations is inconceivable.

The Fragility of Economic Power. In July 1944, at the height of World War II, the foundations for today's International Monetary Fund system were laid at an in-

ternational conference held in the town of Bretton
Woods, New Hampshire. This conference to define the
workings of the world economy in the postwar period
was attended by representatives of the Allied countries,
including John Maynard Keynes of Great Britain and
Harry D. White of the United States. The conference
would not only establish a monetary system, it would
also determine whether the pound or the dollar would
have primacy in the postwar world. By this time the
Allied countries could read the signs of German and
Japanese defeat and had begun to take steps accordingly.

Keynes's concept was that the IMF should act as a
clearinghouse, coordinating and maintaining a balance
so that no particular country would become too weak
or too strong. This, of course, was a desperate attempt
to preserve British authority and save the pound.
White's plan was to place America at the center and
subordinate all the other countries around it like satellites. It tied the dollar to the gold standard and created
a fixed exchange rate for all other currencies. Despite
Keynes's strong opposition to White's plan, there was
no contest between the ascending dollar and the setting sun of the British pound. Keynes's arguments fell
on deaf ears. The key currency shifted from the pound
to the dollar, and world leadership shifted from Great
Britain to the United States.

The present IMF system thus came about in part
through American steamrolling, and America is unlikely to give up control of the IMF unless it is forced to
do so. The IMF was created at a time when America
accounted for 52 percent of the world's Gross National
Product (GNP) and two-thirds of the world's gold sup-

ply. That America with a mere 3 percent of the world's population had so much wealth is amazing. That period was indeed an unprecedented golden age for the United States, which was able to do whatever it pleased.

Despite Keynes's desperate efforts at Bretton Woods, the outcome was inevitable. Britain no longer had the political, economic, or military clout to prevent the dollar from replacing the pound as the key currency. Though it has declined since those heady days, the United States remains a great power. Replacing America today with second-place Japan or Germany would leave much to be desired. But even if these countries were absolute equals with the United States, the transfer of leadership as the result of discussion is inconceivable. History teaches that there has to be some dramatic upheaval for world leadership to shift.

We therefore cannot expect any change in the IMF system until America becomes much weaker and the number-two powers much stronger—and much stronger not only in terms of their economic capabilities. In order to attain superpower status a country also needs physical, that is, military, strength. Economic power is too fragile to respond in emergency situations. In the 1980s Japan went on a shopping spree, buying up America and investing elsewhere overseas. If the laws changed or a war broke out in any of those foreign countries, however, Japan's foreign investments would be frozen or confiscated and that would be the end of that.

At present Japan does not even have the power to protect Japanese corporations that have set up businesses overseas. Take the case of the Iran Japan Petrochemical Company, a joint venture between Iran and members of the Mitsui group. Its plans to build a petrochemical company in southern Iran were interrupted first by the Khomeini revolution and then by the Iran-Iraq war, resulting in the loss of millions of dollars. If Japan had had military capabilities, the results might have been different. Japanese oil tankers sailing into the Persian Gulf would not have had to seek American protection during the Iran-Iraq war. At the very least, there would have been no outcry in the United States about Japan's getting a free ride militarily. More recently during the Gulf War, I repeatedly heard Americans ask why the lives of American young people should be sacrificed to give Japan access to the oil it needs so that it can go on making money. Despite having contributed $13 billion to the war effort, Japan had little say, diplomatically speaking, in the postwar settlement. Most Japanese sense that Japanese diplomacy carries little weight. Does any country look to the prime minister of Japan for leadership? Though it may pride itself on being an economic superpower, Japan is still frustrated by its relative powerlessness on the world scene.

To turn the argument around, it could be said that Japan, which has so little political or military strength, has come to have too much economic power. Having written this, I should hasten to say that I am not a Japanese nationalist or a hawk who wants to see Japan rearm. As a realist I am merely pointing out the obvious. Shintaro Ishihara's statement that Japan might call on Russia to defend it if America tried to contain Japan is nonsense. In such an event, Russian demands are unlikely to stop at microchips. To put it bluntly, as far as most Japanese are concerned, Russia is not the country that they are most likely to trust. The realistic view is that it would be far better for Japan to listen to America's complaints than to join hands with the country that stole Japan's Northern Territories at the end of World War II.

Excessive Exports versus Excessive Imports. In order for the dollar to function as the key currency, America must reconsider its special right to cheap imports and exercise restraint. If it is going to be the world's leader, it must act like a leader and show more self-control. This means becoming more internationally competitive and achieving a trade balance through an export effort or through a further devaluation of the dollar. Competitiveness can be achieved by letting the dollar fall even further, but there is an inherent contradiction in a constantly declining dollar. A key currency that falls unchecked makes no sense as a key currency. Thus, as long as the dollar is the key currency, it must not be allowed to fall indefinitely.

After the Plaza Accord, the dollar plummeted and by 1988 it had reached an exchange rate of 120 yen. At the time some predicted that the dollar might drop even further to the 100-yen or 80-yen level. (At the time this book went to press, the exchange rate was fluctuating between 125 and 104 yen to the dollar.) Although logically speaking it is not strange for the value of the dollar to go down, as a key currency it should not do so. It cannot depreciate so much that it loses its meaning as the key currency. So, in fact, America had no alternative but to become more competitive and increase exports. Since it is impossible to regain overnight something that has been lost over a period of years, the real agenda behind the SII trade talks was to get Japan to import more American goods and to get the United States to import less from Japan.

This put Japan in a peculiar position. Because exports had exceeded imports for some time, Japan had excess reserves that enabled it to import whatever it wanted. It was no longer necessary, as it once had been, to export in order to import. Thus, just as America continues to import even though it can no longer afford to do so, Japan continued to export even though it no longer needed to do so.* This exporting for the sake of exporting is illogical, economically speaking. The more Japan exports, the stronger the yen grows and the more unprofitable exporting becomes. It would make far better sense to spend the money at home. But no effort whatsoever was made to apply the brakes to Japan's export drive. The more Japan exported, the more money came in so that it became even harder to say "stop." What corporation would be willing to cut back exports and reduce tangible profits for the intangible good of the state? The worst aspect of all this is that Japanese society looks up to businessmen as its heroes, and everyone—both inside and outside government—listens to their views. The Recruit scandal and, more recently, the revelation of payments made to leading Diet members by Sagawa Kyubin, a parcel-delivery company, have given a glimpse of how pervasive the practice of influence buying is in Japan, and how deeply politicians are in the pay of business.

---

*Japan's economic growth has reduced the already low level of Japanese imports still further. As imports decline and exports increase (or even remain the same), the trade surplus continues to grow.

America faces a similar dilemma. The fact that the dollar, as the key currency, cannot fall below a certain point, makes it even more difficult to say "stop importing." Paradoxically, what has happened in both Japan and the United States as far as business is concerned is entirely rational economic behavior, and we can only assume that the present situation will continue as long as the IMF system remains unchanged.

Made in Japan—Breaking Down the Exchange Myth. As I mentioned earlier, when the value of the dollar declined by half and the yen doubled, Japanese corporations ended up making exactly the same profits as before. That was odd enough, but the 1985 currency realignment caused another strange phenomenon to occur. American exports to Japan ought, in theory, to have sold for half their former price (provided that demand elasticities were close to unity). This did not happen. At the very least, the curious sight of Japanese bringing back armloads of European goods that they had bought in the United States ought to have disappeared, but the crowds of Japanese shoppers in airport duty-free shops did not diminish at all. In other words, the benefits from the yen's sharp rise against the dollar were not adequately passed on to Japanese consumers. Nor did prices for Japanese goods rise sharply in the United States. Since the value of the dollar was half what it used to be, the prices of Japanese goods ought to have been double what they once were, but that was not the case.

In fact, between 1985 and 1989 the prices of Japanese exports to the United States rose only about 8 to 10 percent despite the fact that the yen had doubled in value. How was that possible? There are two lines of thought on this matter. The first view is that Japanese businesses did not take much of a profit on their exports, that they made their money by setting a high price domestically and holding down export prices to a level where they at least did not sustain a loss. The other view is that, to ride out the strong yen, Japan focused its efforts on restructuring and technological innovation. As a result, costs came down so substantially that there was no need to raise prices.

Although the cheap dollar seemed to offer the United States the perfect opportunity to expand its exports to Japan, it was unable to do so. Why? There are two lines of thought on this question as well. One is that America's export effort was inadequate; the other is that the Japanese market has so many barriers that no matter how hard America tries it cannot get in.

All of these views are probably true. The price of Japanese goods certainly did not double. That is because Japanese business took the loss, and also because they steadily reduced costs and thereby increased their ability to resist the effects of a strong yen. The fact that American exports to Japan did not noticeably increase is due both to the failings of America's own export efforts and to Japan's reluctance to open its market. These overlapping factors formed the background to the Japan–U.S. Structural Impediments Initiative talks.

Yet, while everyone complained that the price of American exports to Japan did not go down in proportion to the yen-dollar exchange rate, even though this proved disadvantageous to the Japanese consumer, everyone blithely accepted the fact that prices for Japanese exports to the United States did not rise much. Properly speaking, the amount of increase or decrease should be symmetrical, and it seems unfair that there was so much hostility to the one and no acknowledgment of the other. After all, if the price of Japanese goods ought to have risen by 100 percent, but Japanese companies kept the increase down to only 8 to 10 percent, they ought to be thanked for their contribution to holding down inflation in the United States. But instead of being grateful, Americans blamed Japan for the fact that U.S. products did not sell for half price in Japan. This is what economics calls asymmetry.

Physical phenomena usually occur symmetrically. If 70 degrees Fahrenheit is the ideal temperature for human beings, then anything higher than 70 degrees is considered hot, anything lower is cold, and discomfort is felt proportionally at the higher or lower temperatures. Although the same ought to hold true for economic phenomena, one extreme was welcomed, the other was decried. That is what makes economics so difficult. It is human nature, of course, to keep silent about something advantageous to one's own pocketbook. The Japanese, however, should have drawn attention to this situation and stated their case firmly, but they remained strangely inarticulate. If Japanese officials and the mass media had made Japan's position better known to the American public, the attitude of ordinary Americans might be considerably different. It would certainly be more beneficial to both countries if the Japanese media concentrated their talents and efforts on giving a clear account of Japan's position rather than producing sensationalist programs like the one mentioned earlier on American racism.

The appreciation of the yen and the devaluation of the dollar after the 1985 Plaza Accord did not have the expected results. The participants now concede that all their tinkering with the exchange rates had almost no effect on imports and exports. Take, for example, the videocassette recorder (VCR). In the beginning neither the Japanese nor the Americans anticipated the size of the market for VCRs. The machines did not sell well at all in the 1970s, but in the early eighties they suddenly became popular, and by 1985 nearly a third of all American households had VCRs, almost all of which were made in Japan. After the Plaza Accord the yen suddenly shot up and the dollar dropped, until ultimately the yen was worth nearly twice what it had been. Logic dictates that the price of Japanese VCRs should have doubled during that period and sales should have dried up. In fact, after 1985 sales of VCRs rose by leaps and bounds, first, because the price did not go up and, second, because American incomes increased greatly after 1985. As a result, Japanese exports of VCRs grew seventeenfold between 1985 and 1990, and by 1989, 75 percent of all American households had a VCR.

One other factor needs to be taken into consideration to account for the failure of the currency realignment to affect sales of VCRs: Japan's virtual monopoly of the VCR market. A monopoly renders the exchange rate mechanism ineffective because the exchange rate can adjust for surpluses and deficits only when substitute products are available from other countries. At present, export figures for VCRs are declining, an indication that the market is mature and that most purchases now are to replace older models. But a situation quite similar to the one for VCRs in the 1980s is evolving in the market for facsimile machines. As in the case of VCRs, Japanese companies have a virtual monopoly on fax machines.

Although, all things being equal, the currency re-evaluations should theoretically have caused the Japanese share of the VCR market to fall from 33 percent to 15 or 16 percent, just the opposite occurred. As American prosperity led to increased absorbability, economies of scale were brought into play and unit costs came down. Meanwhile, to counter the strong yen, Japanese businesses restructured and put greater emphasis on technological innovation and automation that led to wholesale cost reductions. In short, economies of scale and technological innovation made possible low-cost mass production so that Japanese VCR manufacturers were able to achieve a seventeenfold increase in sales despite the adverse climate resulting from the strong yen.

As a result, the Japanese consumer electronics industry achieved an unrivaled position, nearly a monopoly, flooding world markets with goods labeled "made in Japan." Japanese goods earned such enormous profits that the question of who was more at fault for this flood tide—those who import or those who export—ceased to have any relevance. Nothing seemed to be able to check the Japanese export juggernaut. Under the circumstances, what other course was open for America except, as Fallows suggests, to consider the new ploy of containment?

TWO

CONFLICTING VIEWS OF THE ROLE OF GOVERNMENT

Economic Strength as a National Security Issue

Japanese Hypercorporatism. One crucial difference between the United States and Japan is that Japan is a country that holds government in high esteem, whereas the American public has a fundamental distrust of government. This difference is significant because, as many have pointed out, postwar Japan has become an economic superpower under the "administrative guidance" of the Ministry of International Trade and Industry (MITI), the government department whose function is to formulate and implement Japanese commercial and industrial policies. In order to rebuild a country that had been reduced to rubble during World War II, the Japanese government adopted policies that favored production and provided indirect support to help producers maximize their market share. In contrast, a mature capitalist society like the United States tends to regard government intervention in the activities of producers as undesirable and favors policies that improve the well-being of the consumer. In an article in the *Nihon Keizai Shimbun* of September 17, 1990, I called this sort of Japanese capitalism "hypercorporatism" and the mature capitalism of North America and Europe "hyperconsumerism." To adopt the terminology of Alfred Chandler in *Scale and Scope: The Dynamics of Industrial Capitalism,* if the United States is a system of competitive managerial capitalism and Germany is a system of corporate managerial capitalism, then perhaps we might call Japan a state managerial capitalist system.

Spurred by the astonishing prosperity Japan has achieved, some American and European policymakers have begun to advocate a form of government-led capitalism that would provide support to corporations. The reaction in America to industrial policy, however, has been consistently negative. Although Washington has, in fact, stepped in to protect producers on numerous occasions, the American people have a deep-seated, almost physical, aversion to providing systematic protection for particular companies.

In Japan, however, although some of the glitter is gradually wearing off the hypercorporatist system, the Japanese people still have absolute trust in those in positions of authority. The reason everything in Japanese life converges on Tokyo is that that is where the *okami*—the higher powers—congregate and govern their subjects from a position that is above the law. Tokyo's ability to attract those who have an exclusive hold on power and information is prodigious. The city is Washington and New York combined.

In America there is a clear distinction between the functions of those two cities: power is in the hands of the government in Washington; the private sector, based to a large extent but not exclusively in New York, controls information. Power itself is regarded as something that is entrusted by the people to political leaders and can be taken away from them at the first sign of any slip. Deep down Americans have little confidence in government. Mistrust of Washington is particularly deep-rooted among state governments.

This hostility to government is ingrained in the American people. Government service has little appeal for young people. Many of the most gifted undergraduates at American universities go on to pursue advanced degrees in graduate or professional schools; the second-best go to work for major corporations; few of the elite seem interested in a career in government. In contrast, the top graduates of Japan's top university, the University of Tokyo, set their sights on passing the civil service examination and enter the government in droves. The American image of government is one of agencies squabbling with each other over money (a bigger share of the budget), and for that reason the government commands little respect. Recently, I must admit, similar feelings have been gaining ground among the Japanese as well.

In 1989 I had a conversation with a former vice-minister of MITI who asked me an extremely interesting question: "With all this talk about the American economy being on the decline and the United States falling behind in technology, why does the American government stand idly by? Why doesn't it do something? In Japan MITI would have taken action long ago." Although one can understand the vice-minister's perplexity, the United States makes a sharp distinction between the sphere of government and that of the private sector. No matter how frustrated the American government may feel, no matter how much authority it may have, the American people would not tolerate its interfering in private enterprise.

The only areas in which Washington can openly intervene and make policy decisions are those related to military matters and national security. Conversely speaking, if these areas can be used as justification, the government can get involved in anything it wishes. All it has to say is that national security is at stake and those who ordinarily would object will remain silent. National security is the "open sesame" that unlocks all doors. Setting aside what might be done behind the scenes, any top U.S. government official who openly attempts to give public support to a private company will immediately lose his job. What makes James Fallows's proposal for containing Japan so difficult to adopt as a policy measure is that the U.S. government would have to support one corporation or industry over another in order to win the trade war with Japan. Washington, however, cannot openly propose special rules for private corporations.

What then is it to do? When the government chooses to give support to the private sector, it dreams up an excuse for doing so, namely, that such action is necessary for military reasons or in the interest of national security. Once an action can be justified on these grounds, anything is possible. Thus we have seen Fuji-

tsu prevented from buying Fairchild Camera and In-
strument Corporation, the smashing of a Toshiba radio
cassette player on the steps of the Capitol, and Washington's blithe reversal of its own decisions about the
FSX fighter support plane.

Excuses for Japan-Bashing. Each of these incidents was
justified on grounds that came close to pure fabrica-
tion. The reason given by the Commerce Department,
the Defense Department, and the Congress for stop-
ping Fujitsu from buying an 80-percent share of Fairchild in 1987 was that semiconductors are a strategic,
high-tech product and that the takeover of a leading
American semiconductor company by a foreign firm
would pose a serious national security problem. Fairchild was a subsidiary of a French firm, however, and
not an American company at all, to say nothing of the
fact that Schlumberger, its French parent company,
wanted to sell it because of management difficulties.
Yet as soon as national security was invoked, the American government felt it could step in and call the deal
off.

The Toshiba affair was also highly suspect. In 1985
the United States informed the Japanese government
that Toshiba Machine Company, a subsidiary of Toshiba Corporation, had sold precision milling equipment to the Soviet Union in violation of COCOM, the
coordinating committee for controlling East-West
trade. This equipment, it was claimed, had made it
possible for the USSR to reduce the noise of its submarines, thereby making them harder to detect. As a result, the United States had been forced to assume an
additional defense burden of $30 billion. No cause-and-

effect relationship between Toshiba's milling equipment and the noise reduction was ever established, nor was any reliable source ever given for the $30-billion figure. Nevertheless, when the incident was made public in 1987, hawks in the Congress, under the banner of "national security," smashed a Toshiba radio cassette player with sledgehammers on the steps of the Capitol. A Norwegian company, Kongsberg Vaapenfabrikk, had also sold this kind of equipment to the Soviet Union, however, and Russian submarines had become quieter well before the sales by Toshiba Machine began. To put it bluntly, Japan was "had" by then Secretary of Defense Caspar Weinberger.

As for the FSX, Japan was forced to make humiliating concessions in its plans to develop the next generation of support fighters for the Japanese Air Self-Defense Force. By making the FSX into a political issue, America was able to indulge in as much Japan-bashing as it pleased.

Under pressure from Weinberger, in January 1988 Japan abandoned plans to develop its own fighter support plane and agreed to a joint U.S.–Japan development project. That November the two countries exchanged a memorandum of understanding to the effect that Japan would assume the entire cost of the project in exchange for American aviation technology. On January 29, 1989, however, the *Washington Post* carried an article by Clyde Prestowitz entitled "Giving Japan a Handout," which charged that America was giving away its airplane technology to Japan. Although an agreement had been reached the previous year with the Reagan administration and a memo of understanding had already been exchanged, the United States unreasonably demanded that the issue be reopened. The upshot was that America withdrew its promise to furnish "critical" jet engine technology, and the baffling decision was made that Japan was to unconditionally turn over to the United States the technology it had independently developed. At the heart of the issue was America's fear that if it provided Japan with technology, Japan would "beat the United States at its own game" and overtake America in aerospace and defense-related industries as it had in other areas. In the words of *Newsweek* (August 7, 1989), "For the first time, policymakers treated America's economic strength as a national-security issue."

Public hearings on the FSX project were held during the spring of 1989. American congressmen know nothing about Article 9 of the Japanese constitution that forever renounces "war as a sovereign right of the nation and the threat or use of force as a means of settling international disputes." They are equally ignorant of Japan's three principles on weapon exports, first promulgated by Prime Minister Eisaku Sato in 1967, that forbid the export of weapons to communist countries, to countries to which the United Nations prohibits the export of weapons, or to countries that currently are, or might become, involved in international conflict. The purpose of the hearings was to provide an opportunity for U.S. government officials to explain these and other issues and answer any questions.

As I watched the coverage of the hearings on C-SPAN, it was abundantly clear that trade matters and national security issues had become closely linked. The members of Congress bombarded the witnesses with questions. Secretary of Defense Richard Cheney was asked what would happen if Japan diverted the FSX technology the United States was to supply and sold it to the Soviet Union. Cheney replied that there was no cause for concern on that subject because of Japan's peace constitution and its three principles on the export of weapons.

Almost before Cheney had finished answering, another congressman jumped in with the next question. Wasn't it clear that Japan would steal our technology? Didn't the Japanese pose a threat to the supremacy of the American aeronautics industry? Secretary of Commerce Robert Mosbacher answered that he too had been most concerned about that point so he had gone over everything more than once including the black boxing of the essential software. He assured his interlocutor that there was no need to worry. Other questions followed: 60 percent of the procurements were to be awarded to Japanese contractors and only 40 percent to Americans. If America supplied the technology, shouldn't its share be 60 percent? The government's reply was that the Japanese government was putting up all the money for the FSX. Under those circumstances, a 40-percent share for the United States was a "good deal."

Two things became clear from the hearings. First, Cheney and Mosbacher pleaded Japan's case with as much fervor as officials from Japan's Ministry of International Trade and Industry might have done. The American departments of Defense and Commerce were clearly not at variance with MITI and the Japanese Self-Defense Agency on this matter; the problem lay with the U.S. Congress. Moreover, as is the case with politicians in other countries, these congressmen were poorly informed. The fact that votes are more important than issues clearly holds true of legislators on both sides of the Pacific. Secondly, a clear link was forged between trade and national defense. This, of course, is a dangerous precedent because once economics and national defense are linked, Congress may be encouraged to indulge in Japan-bashing in other areas.

There was one amusing incident during these hearings. At one point the representative from Samoa raised his hand and said that he was very upset by the Japan-bashing he had been witnessing. Samoa, he said, had good relations with Japan, which was a valued friend. Some had said that Japan was unfair to foreigners, but one of his relatives, Mr. Konishiki, had just become the sumo champion. The hall erupted with laughter. A black Congressman immediately retorted that Mr. Konishiki might be well treated, but the Japanese were prejudiced against blacks. He was strongly opposed to the FSX deal for Japan because Japanese companies refuse to employ black workers.

As this exchange indicates, the FSX hearings were not limited to a discussion of the FSX. They provided a forum for statements for and against Japan, its fairness or unfairness, that extended ultimately even to matters of race. Although special broadcasts of the public hearings were carried live on cable television, the newspapers and the regular television news programs were highly selective in their coverage and constantly distorted the truth. Even the *New York Times* in an editorial on May 2, 1989, asked why Japan, with its enormous trade surplus, was insisting on developing its own plane rather than buying the F-16 from the United States. Needless to say, no one bothered to report

Cheney's statement that the United States would receive approximately the same benefits from the FSX joint project as it would from selling the F-16, or that the F-16 is not necessarily suited to Japan given the country's limited land space and the vast extent of the territory it must defend. It is easy to understand why the American public, who knew none of the details of the FSX deal and read only patchy accounts of the proceedings, might be led to believe that Japan's development of the FSX posed some sort of a threat to the United States.

Without knowledge of this background, it would be impossible to understand why the appearance of a pirated translation of *The Japan That Can Say "No"* in the late summer and early fall of 1989 created such a furor in the United States.* For America the most important issue of all is national security. *The Japan That Can Say "No"* presented the perfect opportunity to play up that issue. American trade hawks took full advantage of Shintaro Ishihara's boasts about Japan's technological superiority and created a huge sensation. Having won the FSX battle, they now turned their attention to high-definition television technology, which Japan had the lead in developing, and attempted to link it too to national security. Thus, *The Japan That Can*

---

* The Japan That Can Say "No" was published in Japan in January 1989. Based on transcripts of talks given by Akio Morita, chairman of Sony Corporation, and Shintaro Ishihara, a member of the Diet for the supporters of the Liberal Democratic party (LDP), the book consists of five chapters by Morita and five by Ishihara. The authorized English translation, which was published in 1992, contains only the sections by Ishihara, because Morita withheld his consent to the project.

Say "No" provided America with a number of excuses for Japan-bashing. The book was a classic example of how Japan's nationalistic rhetoric can play into the hands of its opponents on this side of the Pacific. It was a tragedy—a minus-sum game—a bad situation for both sides. By no means could it be characterized as zero-sum. Japan lost and so did the United States. When Akio Morita and Shintaro Ishihara, the book's authors, first published the book, neither of them intended, or even suspected, that their book would cause such a stir. The situation was truly absurd.

The Japan That Can Say "No"

Rational and Irrational Policies. Economic policies have their rational and irrational sides. Some are based on reason; others are quite illogical. A glance at postwar America and Japan reveals that logical policies have coexisted with illogical ones in both countries. As far as trade is concerned, Japan's economic policy is extremely rational. In order to expand exports, Japan has boosted competitiveness and offered large quantities of good products at low prices to the rest of the world while making every effort to economize at home and earn foreign currency. This eminently logical policy is Japan's rational approach to foreign trade.

Japan's domestic policies, on the other hand, have been extremely illogical. Good examples are the food control system and the distribution system, both of which reflect a built-in favoritism toward certain interest groups. Even without America making an issue of these policies, it is readily apparent that there is something strange about them. In these areas custom wins out over efficiency, and business is conducted in an opaque and ambiguous manner that international society finds incomprehensible. The rules of competition and all the other principles of modern economic theory simply do not apply.

Under the Staple Food Control Act, for instance, rice cannot be imported into Japan. This law serves both to protect Japanese farmers and to allow Japan to remain self-sufficient in its staple food (see chapter 4), but it also means that the Japanese consumer has to pay several times the world price for rice. A similar situation holds true with regard to the distribution network. Although European goods, for example, are sold at reasonable prices in the American marketplace, as soon as they enter Japan's domestic market, they wind their way through mysterious channels and emerge bearing higher price tags than can be found anywhere else in the world. This is true of Burberry, Gucci, Louis Vuitton, and all the rest. Someone somewhere seems to be making an exorbitant profit, but who?

A country's logical and illogical policies are what I like to think of as its "front door" versus its "back door." If Japan's logical trade policies are viewed as a front door, then its illogical domestic policies are its back door. Japan has kept its main entrance neat and clean for all to see, but its back door is a mess. When the United States finally became aware of this, it began complaining that Japan's dirty domestic policies block America's access to Japanese markets. Its demands for a back door that would give America easier access was what the 1989–90 U.S.–Japan Structural Impediments Initiative talks were all about.

The Japanese themselves, however, do not think their back door is messy or illogical at all. When America points out problem areas in Japan's domestic policy, the Japanese response is "mind your own business." The reason for these policies is the relative homogeneity of Japanese society. In a gemeinshaft society like Japan, where everyone has the same features and the same color skin and where lifestyles and patterns of behavior are similar, the most important policy is to prevent too great a gap from developing between rich and poor and to satisfy as many people as possible by creating a large middle class. To do so, Japan liberally protects farmers, maintaining price supports for rice and paying out subsidies to reduce the acreage under cultivation no matter how illogical these measures may be. It also protects mom-and-pop stores by limiting the size and number of new stores under the Large-Scale Store Law (see chapter 4) no matter how much this may violate the workings of market mechanisms. As a result, Japan has succeeded in creating a country with a population of more than 120 million people, all of whom belong to the middle class. What is wrong with that? Japan asks.

This type of reasoning is incomprehensible in the United States, however, which has a healthy consumers' movement and an efficient market system based on the principle of offering quality products at reasonable prices. To return to our earlier metaphor, this is America's front entrance, which it keeps neat and well swept. But America, too, has a back door, its foreign policy, the irrationality of which is particularly noticeable in the areas of diplomacy, national defense, and trade. For example, the United States regards the countries of Central America as its backyard. It sends its troops there whenever it pleases and has even arrested the leader of one country and forcibly carried him off to America to stand trial without thinking twice about it. It provides arms and money and abets antigovernment guerrillas in countries that are unfriendly to the United States and has no scruples about doing other things that most Japanese find equally shocking. No matter how illogical these acts seem to Japan, many Americans regard them as right and just and a reflection of American prestige. A foreign policy success in America has traditionally translated into a sudden rise in a president's popularity ratings. According to a January 1990 Gallup poll, after General Manuel Noriega had been taken prisoner in Panama, President Bush's approval rating soared to 80 percent. In March 1991, after the successful conclusion of the Gulf War, it reached an unprecedented 89 percent.

Thus both Japan and the United States have their logical and illogical sides. In Japan the logical side is the face it shows to the rest of the world; the illogical side is its domestic policies. In America the situation is just the opposite. Until recently this has worked very much to Japan's advantage. Japan's front door—exporting—has matched perfectly with America's front door—domestic consumption. As a result, Japanese exports have expanded enormously, and U.S. consumers have been able to enjoy large quantities of high-quality, low-priced goods. Up till now Japan has also been lucky because America's illogical side has not had much effect on Japan since it has been directed toward countries, the Soviet Union in particular, that have been ideological opponents of the American system.

The American attitude toward communism has long seemed quite irrational to outside observers. In the past, whenever news unfavorable to the Soviet Union was reported, the reaction was "See? Russia really is evil. We must fight communism." This only caused anticommunist sentiment to escalate even further. Whenever I encountered instances of this irrational antipathy, I would think to myself, "The Soviet Union isn't really as bad as all that. How frightening it would be if Japan were regarded in this way." In 1989 these fears seemed about to materialize. Although Japan had managed to avoid provoking American wrath in areas involving U.S. national security or military affairs, during the mid to late 1980s the situation began to take an ominous turn. As the Soviet Union became less of a threat, America began to link economics with national security. Just as the USSR had been branded the "evil empire," Japan was being branded as "unfair." Whenever reports were published about bid rigging for construction projects or computer companies that submitted winning bids of one yen for long-term municipal contracts, a chorus of voices greeted the news with "See? Japan is unfair." The result of tossing a book as inflammatory as *The Japan That Can Say "No"* into this potentially explosive atmosphere was all too clear.

Why The Japan That Can Say "No" *Provoked American Wrath.* When *The Japan That Can Say "No"* came out in Japan in January 1989, neither of its authors foresaw the controversy their comments would cause. After all, in the past, many critics had made statements similar to theirs with impunity. But in the early fall of 1989 problematic passages from the book were translated and distributed throughout the U.S. Congress. A pirated translation was subsequently circulated around the country via fax machines and electronic mail networks. Contributing to the book's notoriety was the fact that one of the authors, Akio Morita, chairman of Sony Corporation, is synonymous with "Japan Inc." and the other, Shintaro Ishihara, a member of the Diet for the Liberal Democratic party (LDP), was described as a prominent politician. It is not strange that congressmen as well as ordinary Americans, who know little about Japanese politics, might mistakenly believe that Ishihara was a politician of considerable stature in Japan. In fact, Ishihara was later compared to Richard Gephardt and Morita to Lee Iacocca. Since these two important people had made these statements against America, it was perhaps only natural for Americans to assume that all Japanese must think the same thing.

Some of the blame for the controversy lies with the Japanese publishing world, which has a predilection for cheap, sensationalist titles that, like tabloid headlines, seem to hint at some big scoop. *The Japan That Can Say "No"* is a clever title from a marketing point of view, but considering the harm it did to U.S.–Japanese relations, it was a little like killing the goose that laid the golden eggs. As in the case of James Fallows and "Containing Japan," for Morita and Ishihara too, the title of their book took on a significance of its own, quite independent of its contents, and caused all sorts of problems. To be sure, the book contained disquieting statements, but if it had been published under a different title, *Proposals for U.S.–Japan Relations,* for example, it would most likely not have provoked much of a reaction.

When the Morita-Ishihara book first created a stir in

When the Morita-Ishihara book first created a stir in the United States, Japanese misunderstood what the fuss was about and jumped to the conclusion that Americans were reacting to the book's title. This provoked a backlash in the opposite direction. What was so wrong, Japanese asked, about Japan saying "no"? Does America have the right to expect Japan to do everything its way? What had upset America, however, was not the possibility that Japan might say "no." In fact, the United States would greatly welcome a clear "yes" or "no" from Japan, instead of the vague, noncommittal responses that Japanese officials are all too prone to make. A good case in point was the U.S.–Japan agreement in August 1991 to increase the foreign share of the Japanese semiconductor market to 20 percent by the end of 1992. When the goal was not reached by that date (it was, in fact, achieved in March 1993), the Japanese side responded that the 20-percent figure had been a target at which to aim, not a goal that they were committed to fulfill. This inability or unwillingness to give a definite answer has created a climate in which misunderstanding thrives and has driven America to complain that negotiating with Japan is somewhat akin to peeling an onion—responses are always piecemeal and one obstacle follows another ad infinitum. When Japan means "no" it should say "no," and when it means "yes" it should say "yes." America would have no serious objections to that.

The problem lies in what Japan might say "no" to. On issues related to America's national defense and security, Japanese should be very cautious about even hinting, as Shintaro Ishihara did, that Japan might bypass the United States and enter into friendly relations with the Soviet Union or that it might use its superior technology as a trump card in negotiating a trade deal. Statements in *The Japan That Can Say "No"*—such as "Japan's technology has advanced so much, that Americans get hysterical"; or "If . . . Japan sold [computer] chips to the Soviet Union and stopped selling them to the United States, this would upset the entire military balance"—had the effect of salt rubbed into a wound with a scrubbing brush, and they inevitably provoked American rage.

Some may ask why it is wrong to tell America the truth. I would answer that it is not the whole truth. Although the technological strengths of the two countries are converging, comparisons of which country is ahead and which lags behind can be made only in certain areas. Japan may have outstripped the United States in these areas, but if it fails to grasp the full picture of America's national strength, it is not seeing the forest for the trees. To say Japan should not be intimidated by the United States is all well and good, but no advantage whatsoever can be gained by worsening U.S.–Japan relations nor is there any need to annoy America simply for annoyance's sake.

A striking example of the reaction the book provoked was the op-ed article that economist Lawrence Summers, a middle-of-the-roader who personifies American good sense, wrote for the *New York Times* (December 3, 1989) which began "Dear Mr. Morita and Mr. Ishihara":

Most American economists, myself included, reflexively oppose any sort of policy proposal that interferes with free domestic and international markets. Your new book, "The Japan That Can Say 'No,'" shakes my faith. . . . You both make it clear that Japan's strategy has not been one of maximizing the consumer's gains from trade.... Instead, economically, financially and technologically, Japan has tried—and succeeded in—converting the Japanese-American relationship from one of Japanese dependence to one of mutual dependence. You make it all too clear that the risk, from an American viewpoint, is that before too long, the United States will depend heavily on Japan, but it will not be mutual.

Summers then went on to outline the steps he felt were needed to counter this perceived threat: saving more and investing more in America's physical and human capital; supporting efforts to maintain a viable semiconductor industry to obviate "the risk posed by America's dependence on a supplier of vital military parts whose leaders openly threaten a cutoff"; cultivating the newly industrialized economies of Asia; and aggressively confronting Japanese mercantilism.

Summers's letter concluded:

I do not know what motivated you to write "The Japan That Can Say 'No,'" but I am glad you did. You have helped remind an excessively complacent economics profession that some things like national security are more important than good jobs at good wages. And I suspect your America bashing may have made a stronger case for a new American policy toward Japan than any American ever could.

How should we interpret this profoundly ironic letter that reveals such a deep distrust of Japan? Lawrence Summers is one of the rising stars of American economics. He is also a well-respected figure in political circles, who served as economic adviser to Michael Dukakis during the 1988 presidential campaign and is currently undersecretary of the treasury for international affairs in the Clinton administration.

Summers has always avoided sensationalism and is noted for his sensible statements and calm, dispassionate manner. But the tone of his letter was that of a man seething with rage. As an acquaintance of his, I was profoundly shocked when I read what he had written. When it comes to matters of national security even sensible scholars like Summers share the national belief that money making should take a back seat to national security and that military matters must take precedence over economic concerns. Despite the strong temptation to sell Coca-Cola and Pepsi Cola to the Soviet Union, for years America denied economic logic on the grounds that such sales would boost the Soviet economy and affect U.S. national security. Now that Russia has relinquished its role as The Enemy, hamburger shops have opened in Moscow.

What would happen if Japan were to move into the position that Russia has vacated? No matter how inexpensive or well-made Japanese products might be, Americans, if they thought that enriching Japan would threaten their national security, would flatly repudiate economic principles. Such a backlash might well develop into a boycott against all Japanese products, not just those made by Sony and Toshiba. This sort of response is not confined to the United States alone, however. During World War II, Japan lived in an irrational world of its own, vilifying British and American "devils" and vowing to suppress all personal desires until after Japan had won the war.

The Secret of "Made in Japan"

National Security as "Public Good." It is difficult to reach a political consensus in America, unless, as I have already noted, an action is justified on the grounds of national security. A closer examination of this proposition inevitably leads to the question "what is the role of government?" Since the days of Adam Smith and David Ricardo this question has been a subject of debate among economists. One of the answers that the various schools of thought on this issue have come up with is this: The role of government is service to the people.

Taxes are a means to this end, not an end in themselves. In Japan, *nozei,* the word that means *paying taxes,* still conjures up the image of taxes as something paid as tribute to a feudal overlord, but in America, where democracy has flourished since the country's founding, the word *taxpayer* implies that taxes are paid by each individual citizen in return for services rendered by the state. In other words, the citizen who pays taxes is a customer to whom the government provides special services that cannot be provided by private enterprise. Because government services are meant for all the people, they cannot be the personal property of a particular individual. The government provides "public" goods and services.

One of the first people to popularize the expression "public goods" or "social goods" was Harvard professor emeritus Richard Musgrave in his book *The Theory of Public Finance: A Study in Public Economics.* Musgrave's theory is based on the idea that there are "public wants" and "public goods" and that the government's role is to fill public wants with goods and services. This theory is part of the mainstream of American thought on such matters and has provided an extremely important starting point for thinking about the activities of government. If it is not the role of government to provide private goods, then it logically follows that government should not support, or intervene in, private enterprise. When the U.S. government considers giving its support to something, the inevitable starting point for any discussion is whether a public good or a private good is involved. Thus America, unlike Japan, finds it difficult to adopt an industrial policy and, if forced to do so, must make some arbitrary connection with a public good such as national security. The Japanese government is not concerned about whether something is a public or a private good. Government agencies band together to protect the weak, rushing to the rescue of rice producers, coal mining, or the aluminum industry. This is a major difference between U.S. and Japanese concepts of government and government policy.

What precisely is the difference between a public good and a private good? A private good is one that a particular person pays for with the intention of making it personal property and thereby causing it to come under his or her private ownership. The very fact of ownership means that it cannot belong to anyone else. This is what is known as "the exclusion principle." The goods to which this principle applies are private goods.

Conversely, public goods are those to which the exclusion principle does not apply, those which belong to all the people or which no amount of money can transform into personal property. Thus, when the American government tries to adopt a policy, the exclusion principle has the potential to raise problems. A policy to which the exclusion principle does not apply is easy for Washington to justify as a public good, but it would have a hard time defending a policy to which this principle does apply, one that provides benefits only for the people who pay for it. The existence of the exclusion principle is a serious problem, the dimensions of which are hard for Japanese to conceive.

For these reasons, it is understandable that in the United States the most readily identifiable public good is national defense. Because defending the security of America is the single most important service the government provides, no American citizen can say "no" to it. This is the reason national security policies are enacted fairly easily. Industrial policies, however, encounter serious obstacles because industrial policy is an area where the exclusion principle is apt to operate.

The distinction between public and private goods also helps to account for the American reaction to *The Japan That Can Say "No."* If that book had limited itself to a discussion of industry and had not mentioned American defense, it probably would not have provoked much of a backlash in the United States, despite the caustic nature of its criticisms. By referring to a public good like defense, however, it made Americans' blood boil.

The negative reaction to the statements made by Shintaro Ishihara was clearly stronger than the response to what Akio Morita of Sony had to say. This was due to the fact that Morita's criticisms were about private goods whereas Ishihara's were about public goods. Morita made some scathing comments—Japanese companies look ten years ahead, U.S. companies ten minutes ahead; America claims to be a country that protects human rights but it lays off workers as soon as business is bad, and so forth. Since these barbs were directed at industry, however, Americans were willing to listen. Even if the comments rubbed them the wrong way, Americans could react rationally and say "well said" without any of Lawrence Summers's irony. When it comes to such matters, the American sense of fair play clearly comes to the fore. But Ishihara's criticisms touched on national security, and that's a different ball game.

The Perception Gap over Defense. The concept of public goods can be used to shed some light on the true nature of the clash between the United States and Japan over defense. Back in 1981, then Prime Minister Zenko Suzuki announced that Japan would protect the commercial sea lanes up to a thousand nautical miles from Japan. This decision was made to ensure the free movement of vital imports, especially oil from the Persian Gulf. At the time, however, the United States was particularly concerned with the movement of Soviet submarines through the Sea of Japan on their way to the Pacific Ocean from their base at Vladivostok. Aspart of its military strategy vis-à-vis the Soviet Union, it wanted the Japanese to assume responsibility for their maritime self-defense. When relations between America and Japan began to deteriorate and disputes flared up in a wide variety of issues, the flames quickly spread to the area of defense. The United States claimed that Japan was enjoying a free ride under the

U.S.–Japan security treaty. It was not paying its fair share but was pouring its energies instead into trade and money making.

Japan interpreted this criticism as merely an extension of the commercial frictions existing between the two countries—America, frustrated in the areas of investment and trade, was now finding fault with Japan in the area of defense. But this view is fundamentally mistaken. Keeping the sea lanes open is clearly an international public good and because the United States and Japan both share in the benefits, they should both contribute their share of the cost of protecting them. Similarly, the service provided under the U.S.–Japan security treaty is an international public good, and that fact naturally puts it in a different sphere than beef, oranges, automobiles, or VCRs. Although countries may bargain about public goods, such bargaining ought not to be construed as friction of the sort that arises in trade disputes over private goods.

Imagine a park, for example. This park is clearly a public good for the particular area in which it is located. No individual can make it his or her personal property, yet he or she and everyone else can use it freely without paying money. The park is, therefore, a public good to which the exclusion principle does not apply. When a park is being created at neighborhood expense, however, troubles may arise over how to allocate shares of the cost. If everyone were perfectly honest, there would be no difficulty, but human beings are fallible. Some will claim they are too poor to contribute; others that they have no children and thus won't use the park. That is where bargaining comes in.

There are two ways to determine who pays what in

such a situation. The first is based on the ability to pay; the second is the benefit approach. Using the first approach, a wealthy person would be asked to pay one thousand dollars; a poor person would be asked for one hundred dollars. In the second scenario, a household with five children would pay five hundred dollars; a household with one child would pay one hundred dollars. Broadly speaking, these are the two methods for determining each person's share. But because there will always be holdouts or those who try to pass the responsibility on to others, some sort of bargaining is inevitable. Thus, there is an inherent weakness associated with the problem of determining who should provide public goods.

By contrast, when private goods are bought and become someone's property, the only potential problem is the ability to pay. There is no bargaining game as in the case of public goods, only endless friction over whether to buy or not buy, sell or not sell, and over who owes what to whom. Insofar as the U.S.–Japan security treaty is an international public good, bargaining about each side's share of the defense costs is only natural. When America says, "Japan is getting a free ride," Japan responds, "That's not true. Our peace constitution and three principles against exporting weapons bind us hand and foot so that we cannot move an inch. Instead, we will pay our share of the expenses for American troops in Japan and buy fighter planes." This is bargaining. It is intrinsic to any public good and must never be confused with trade disputes over exports. It is, therefore, a mistake to confuse public goods with private goods and interpret defense as just another area of friction between the United States and

Japan. Bargaining over defense issues will always exist regardless of whether or not there are trade disputes.

Looked at in this light, Japan's $13-billion contribution to the Gulf War effort might be called its share in the costs of an international public good. The reason Americans were so annoyed by Japan's dilatory response to the contribution question was their belief that, given Japan's ability to pay and its role as a beneficiary of oil from the Persian Gulf, it should have been only natural for Japan to make an immediate decision to assume a large share of the costs.

During the Gulf War, even some Japanese began to have second thoughts about Japan's parochial attitude toward foreign policy. If, as we saw in chapter 1, in a world of growing economic interdependence, it is impossible for one country to grow rich while others fail to prosper, it is becoming equally impossible to remain on the sidelines in international disputes. If the idea that there can be prosperity in one country without prosperity everywhere else reflects Japan's egocentric attitudes toward economics and technology, then the belief that many Japanese seemed to have during the Gulf War that there could be peace in one country regardless of what was happening in the rest of the world reflects a similar egocentrism in foreign affairs. The Japanese government's decision in the summer of 1992 to send members of the Self-Defense Force to Cambodia as part of a UN peace-keeping mission, the first Japanese troops to be sent abroad since World War II, seems to signal a greater willingness on the part of Japan to shoulder more of the military as well as the monetary burdens of the international public good.

Why Can't the United States Adopt an Industrial Policy?
Although, as we have seen, it is difficult for the American government to adopt policies that do not involve public goods, one should not conclude that Washington gives absolutely no support to private goods. Support to private companies would, of course, provoke a huge backlash from the American people, but the government spends vast sums of money on welfare and other areas that are not public goods per se, including Social Security, aid to individuals such as the elderly and the disabled, and aid for disadvantaged or minority groups. The failure of the Democratic party to win a presidential election during the 1980s is generally attributed to popular discontent over all the money spent on these causes during earlier Democratic administrations.

Why are the American people so generous? The answer can be traced back to the humanistic tradition of Western thought. America moves back and forth between the theory of public goods, on the one hand, and the ideals of humanism, on the other, sometimes mixing the two, sometimes keeping them completely separate. This is impossible for Japanese to understand. They find it strange that, despite all the complaints about the erosion of the American economy, the United States has made no effort to adopt a national industrial policy. They find it equally strange that when the Soviet Union refused to let Jews emigrate or the Chinese suppressed protests in Tiananmen Square, Americans were quick to complain about the infringement of human rights and the lack of regard for the individual in these countries, while doing nothing for the homeless in their own land. Or at least that is how it looks to the Japanese.

In grossly oversimplified terms, the people who typify American humanism are the progressives, primarily Democrats, who advocate aiding the disadvantaged. Perhaps not surprisingly, one of the first projects Bill Clinton set in motion upon becoming president was an overhaul of the health care system. The conservatives, mainly Republicans, are supporters of the theory of public goods: They believe that while aid is a good thing, too much of it may deprive people of the will to work. These two concepts, or a combination thereof, take turns guiding American public policy. Corporate activities have no place in this scheme of things because they fall somewhere between the two. The Republican party is generally viewed as speaking for industry. For many Americans, however, industry has a bad image. It is seen as the source of pollution and as being interested only in making money. As a result, many people feel that its activities should be closely scrutinized. This is another reason America cannot adopt a strong industrial policy.

In Japan if something will help the country's exports—be it a public good or a private good, defense related or consumer oriented—government, industry, and academia band together to develop the product and ship it out to markets around the world once it has been perfected. These groups cooperate because it is in the national interest of Japan to do so. From America's perspective this Japanese brand of capitalism is quite "different." Although both America and Japan are capitalist countries, the principles they are based upon are in fact very different: Water and oil are both liquids, but they are very different substances.

The classic example of Japanese industrial policy is the development of color television, which is often cited in courses at American business schools. As Christopher Freeman notes in his book *The Economics of Industrial Innovation:* "Japanese manufacturers were the first to introduce integrated circuit technology into the colour television industry (with the important economies in assembly labour that it involved). The success of this innovation was based on a joint re-search effort starting in 1966 and involving five television manufacturers, seven semiconductor manufacturers, four universities and two research institutes and the overall backing of MITI." That is how things are "made in Japan."

In America this sort of collaboration is inconceivable. Any such project would face two huge obstacles. Suppose, for example, that the American government decided to develop a new computer and called upon five large corporations to work on the project. Because the corporations would develop the computer with taxpayers' money and would also receive other forms of financial assistance, they would probably be quite willing to participate. So far so good. But what would happen when they succeeded in developing the computer and reached the stage of unveiling the new product? Small and medium-sized companies, not to mention the other large companies that had not been asked to join the development group, would not stand idly by. Incensed that preferential treatment had been given to other companies, they would sue the government. After an enormous expenditure of time and money, the court would render its verdict; high-ranking government officials would be fired; and the affair would become a huge scandal.

Even if this first obstacle could be overcome, the quality of the engineers who would be assembled for the project would pose a second stumbling block. In Japan the participating companies would commit their best engineers to such a project. In America the opposite would more than likely happen. The American companies would send only their second- or third-rate engineers because the ones to reap the benefit of the new technology would not be the companies but the individual engineers who participated in developing it. The engineers whose research and development efforts were successful would be free to quit their original employers and take the new technology with them, either to join a rival firm or to set up companies of their own. Because American companies cannot afford to let this happen, they would send their second- or third-rate engineers, and the chances of success would be pretty slim. Since any American joint development project can expect to encounter these two obstacles, the United States will never be able to adopt the kind of industrial policy that exists in Japan.

As long as the United States adheres to the two major principles of humanism and public goods, it cannot openly adopt an industrial policy. For America to set up an equivalent of MITI that would support private goods and favor producers over consumers would be even more out of the question. If Japan believes that the producer comes first, in America it is the consumer who comes first.

For these reasons, any industrial policy that the

United States adopts must somehow be involved with national defense or areas such as space, rockets, and aeronautic technology that are reflections of national prestige. The fact that industrial policy in America is limited to the sphere of public goods whereas industrial policy in Japan is free to cover private goods has unquestionably benefited Japan in the free-trade system and helped bring about America's decline. America's response has been twofold: first, the Structural Impediments Initiative, a list of over two hundred items that America presented to Japan with the demand that Japan play by the same rules; and, second, the threat to abolish the free-trade system and adopt a policy of managed trade. When all is said and done, however, the economic frictions between the United States and Japan are merely the discordant notes produced by a clash between two societies—one that bands together to give priority to the pursuit of money, the other that achieves unity through the pursuit of its own highest priority, power.

Why Japan's Industrial Policy Has Succeeded. In thinking about why Japan's industrial policy has been so successful, there is one other point to consider—the practice of targeting. A major factor contributing to success in any area, not just industrial policy, is having goals. Japan's industrial policy has succeeded because it has had clear goals and because Japanese industry, government, and academia have joined forces in an effort to achieve them. What has motivated the nation is that Japan is number two as a global economic power and has always been tempted by the possibility of becoming number one.

Japan has been given a goal for which it is innately suited—that of providing better goods more cheaply to the rest of the world. It has used the practice of targeting to its advantage in manufacturing color television sets, automobiles, VCRs, and a range of other products. To use the analogy of Richard Zeckhauser, my colleague at Harvard, the situation could be compared to a bicycle race. In a bicycle race it is extremely difficult for the lead rider to hang on to the number one spot. He can't see the riders in back of him, and he receives the full brunt of the wind. The number two rider, following right behind, has it much easier. The most skillful riders, therefore, stick closely behind the lead rider and make a sprint to the finish.

In formulating a successful industrial policy, whether you are in the number one or number two spot makes an enormous difference. The conditions under which an industrial policy can operate effectively favor the country in the number two position and make it difficult for the leading country to even launch such a policy. If in the future Japan should ever actually become the world's premier economic power, the industrial policy that it has been following would no longer work so well for one obvious reason: Japan will no longer be able to practice targeting.

For some time now Japanese companies have been targeting existing American products and manufacturing higher-quality versions. Japan has been particularly efficient about observing America's failures so as to avoid making the same mistakes. If Japan were at the top, however, this strategy would no longer work. Targeting is much talked about these days. But even if America were to adopt an industrial policy like Japan's that involved private goods, since the United States is already number one, it would be hard pressed to know what to develop or how to develop it. Given such uncertain prospects, the government would have trouble justifying the use of taxpayers' money and thus would find it better to leave the whole thing to private enterprise. This sort of thinking makes adopting an industrial policy in the United States even more difficult. Perhaps that is the fate of being number one.

In Japan the situation is just the opposite. The risks are too great to entrust the matter to the private sector. The government must lend a helping hand. Moreover, the Japanese people are by no means opposed to big business. The technology that is developed with the government's help is made available to all companies. The objective is "Japan Inc." and exports. That is the advantage of being number two. As far as industrial policy is concerned, being number one is a tremendous handicap, and that is why America cannot make a bold initiative.

THREE

THE ANATOMY OF U.S.–JAPANESE ANTAGONISMS

American Misconceptions about Japan

America Is a Country of Rules. As I travel back and forth between Japan and the United States, I always feel that the first country is too homogeneous and the second is too pluralistic. In Japan, for example, it is easy to chat with the cab driver on the way to Narita Airport. From the opening conversational gambit about the weather to queries about my destination, the conversation flows smoothly and naturally with no hesitations or awkward silences. A dozen or so hours later when my plane lands in America and I disembark, I again take a taxi. My first thought as I get in is "Is it safe to ride in this cab?" The next is "What sort of person is this cab driver? Will he try to overcharge me?" Tired after the long flight, I am particularly sensitive to the difference between my taxi experiences in Japan and those in

America—between being able to relax and carry on an ordinary conversation and having to be wary and watchful in dealing with the cab driver.

I have been traveling between the United States and Japan on a regular basis for more than thirty years, but I have never become inured to this feeling. Most taxicab drivers in New York and Washington are immigrants. A few may be native born, but the majority are from places like India, Puerto Rico, or Egypt. They often speak with such strong foreign accents that I cannot understand what they are saying. Because we have no common topic of conversation and share no feelings of affinity, a sense of guardedness inevitably prevails in our dealings with one another. This is not necessarily because I am Japanese. Everyone in the United States has his or her own culture and lifestyle, and one cannot expect Americans to communicate with each other as easily as Japanese do.

The idea that Japan is somehow different has currently become popular in America; it would be more appropriate to say that Japan is too much the same. Few countries are as homogeneous as Japan. The United States, on the other hand, is the most diverse country in the world; no culture is more varied. Now that these two countries, which are so diametrically opposite from one another, have begun to call each other odd, it will not be easy for them to find a common ground.

In Japan it is commonly accepted that Japan is inhabited by people whose ancestors from time immemorial were also Japanese. The Japanese—and perhaps only the Japanese—tend to think that just as Japanese live in Japan, "Americans" live in America.

The "Americans" that the Japanese have in mind are those people whose ancestors came over on the *Mayflower* or the Native Americans who were once masters of the American continent. The truth is, of course, that the United States is a country where people of a seemingly infinite variety of ethnic backgrounds and cultures mix together to form what has been called a "salad bowl" and that an American is anyone who has U.S. citizenship. If the Hispanic population continues to increase at the current rate, someday more than half the U.S. population may not speak English. This sort of thing is beyond the comprehension of most Japanese. How ironic that a nation that is composed of many different races and that freely absorbs minor differences should call Japan "different."

Naturally, rules are necessary in a community of such diversity. And those rules must be absolutely explicit. Bringing together people of different cultural, linguistic, and religious backgrounds and divergent lifestyles demands rules that are perfectly clear to everyone. They cannot be understandable only to people of Italian or Spanish descent but must act as the greatest common denominator for people of all backgrounds and help to level their differences. They must be based on the premise that they will be universally intelligible and universally obeyed. The rights and obligations of American citizens are set down in the Constitution. Contracts govern interactions between individuals. This dependence on written codes of behavior is what I mean when I say "America is a country of rules."

In contrast, Japan is a country without an explicit set of rules or, perhaps more accurately, a country that does not need such rules. In a homogeneous society, where complete understanding can be achieved through monosyllables, the rules governing communication and other ordinary activities do not need to be set down in writing or even explicitly articulated. Someone who submits a contract to be signed or proposes a set of rules to be followed runs the risk of being frowned upon for "alien" or "unsociable" behavior. In general, Japanese feel strongly that it is a not a virtue to prescribe rules. This is a major difference between the United States and Japan.

Japanese also feel more comfortable with vagueness and ambiguity than Americans do. When American children study English in school, they are always urged to "be precise" and "use the exact word." Clarity and precision in the expression of ideas may be considered virtues for the speaker or writer of English, but they are not prized by the speaker or writer of Japanese. Out of respect for the feelings of others, Japanese have a strong tendency to put themselves in the other person's position, to try to imagine how he or she might feel, and then to gear their own speech and behavior to fit these views. Avoiding forthright assertions of opinions is a traditional strategy for preventing conflict in a homogeneous society. This preference for oblique forms of expression is reflected in the Japanese language, which does not normally specify gender or number or require that sentences have definite subjects and thus lends itself perfectly to an indirect approach. In international exchanges, however, vague responses that mean neither "yes" nor "no" are no longer acceptable. Japanese negotiators must be able to take a firm stand and present their case convincingly to the American side.

America is a notoriously litigious society. People go to court on any pretext to settle a dispute. In Japan, on the other hand, arbitration is the preferred method for resolving disagreements. Settling an issue once and for all by completely crushing the opponent is not regarded as admirable behavior even by the victor. Out-of-court settlements, mediation, and compromise—each motivated by a spirit of conciliation—are typically Japanese ways of resolving conflicts. Although this attitude seems to be gradually changing, the underlying belief that litigation is somehow not entirely proper still remains. Americans, however, will marshal all the forces at their disposal behind an argument in an all-out effort to win. A conciliatory spirit signifies lack of effort.

If in Japan it is considered bad form to argue, in the United States arguing in the process of reaching an agreement is both the fair way to settle a dispute and a sign of good faith. Seen in this light, the various pressures brought to bear on Japan, such as the Super 301 clause and the Gulf War contributions question, have not been instances of Japan-bashing but rather attempts to make Japan do the "right" thing according to American sensibilities. Although Japan should not overreact to these pressures, it sometimes does. In addition, Japanese bureaucrats and politicians sometimes do not understand what America really wants Japan to do.

The fact that the Japanese are not accustomed to arguing has certainly been a major handicap in exchanges between Japan and the United States. From childhood, Americans have been taught to convince others of the rightness of their assertions and feel no discomfort in doing so. Because this is not the Japanese way, it tends to confuse Japanese officials, who then give a confused response when confronted by American demands. Japanese officials have often bungled things because they are unfamiliar with the negotiating process. Overreacting to American attacks about how different Japan is, they have been known to make statements such as "the Japanese people can't eat too much beef because their intestines are too long" and are then forced into an even more untenable position when the American side responded, "Then, the Japanese are different not only in the way they think but physiologically as well?" Given its propensity to make absurd remarks like these, it is no wonder that the Japanese side is not taken seriously when it tries to make the quite valid point that America's trade deficit would still not go down even if Japan acceded to all America's demands.

The U.S. government wants Japan to be "fair" and to "play by the same rules." It must also convince Congress and ultimately the American people that it is succeeding in these efforts. As the world heads steadily toward a single global market, the game cannot be played if the rules are different from one country to another. The United States, to use a popular image, has said that Japan should not get into the boxing ring wearing only a *fundoshi* (loincloth) and attempt to wrestle sumo-style.

In the past, diplomats needed only to speak each other's language, but that is no longer the case. Today's diplomats have to be tough negotiators. Unfortunately, Japanese diplomats are not provided with this sort of training. For the most part, they are gentlemen who speak excellent English; in other words, they are language-oriented diplomats of the old school. Thus, whenever Japanese–U.S. relations start to unravel, bureaucrats from MITI or the Ministry of Finance must invariably step in. This confuses their American counterparts.

Ministries and agencies in Japan operate independently of one another. With a few exceptions, Japanese bureaucrats do not move from one ministry to another in the course of their careers. Just as a Japanese businessman remains with one company throughout his working life, a civil servant stays in one branch of the government until retirement. This system inculcates an intense loyalty to one's ministry that can often lead to open conflicts with other ministries in areas where interests overlap. If one ministry encroaches upon the rights and privileges of another, a tense situation is likely to develop. When Japan negotiates with America, there is a flurry of activity, and after some fierce infighting between MITI and the Ministry of Finance, the Ministry of Foreign Affairs often gets pushed out into the cold. Members of the Diet can also become involved. As a result, the American side often does not know with whom it should negotiate.

Japanese officials, for their part, sometimes use *gaiatsu,* or "foreign pressure," to their advantage. Policymakers, for example, may secretly desire the reform of certain traditional practices, such as restrictions on rice imports to protect domestic rice farmers, and are glad to meet American demands. Publicly, however, the officials object to the demands, using the United States as a scapegoat, to give the appearance that the reform is being forced upon Japan by international pressures alone.

"Me" Society versus "We" Society. Every society has unwritten rules that govern life in that society. Who makes those rules? Generally speaking, the behavior of the people that society holds in highest esteem serves as the basis for the rules of that society. In America and Japan, however, the rules originate from fundamentally different groups.

Japanese rules are clearly "made in Tokyo," the center of Japan's political, economic, and cultural life. Rules and trends originate there and eventually spread through the rest of the country. This means the rules are progressive as far as the rest of the country is concerned, but conservative for the more radical elements of Tokyo society. An obvious example is provided by the rules of marriage. Today, in both Tokyo and the rest of the country, love matches have replaced arranged marriages as the social norm. This custom clearly originated in Tokyo. Several years ago marrying for love was considered vulgar in the countryside. Those who wished to escape this rule eloped to Tokyo, where love matches were socially acceptable. As the practice of marrying for love began to spread throughout the country, the more progressive couples in Tokyo began to live together without getting married. This practice has yet to be universally accepted, even in Tokyo. My point is that, for the most part, Japan's rules are decided in a particular area, namely, the city of Tokyo.

By contrast, although trends tend to develop in major U.S. cities, especially those along the East and West coasts, particular groups of progressive people make the rules in America rather than one particular progressive place as in Japan. In the matter of marriage, living together before marriage has become accepted behavior among well-educated Americans. Many people in respectable positions in the United States live with their prospective spouses before they get married. This practice is widespread and has none of the taint attached to common-law marriages in Japan. Because it has been socially acceptable for the past decade or so, the couple quite normally attends even the most formal social functions together. While this progressive behavior is displayed by the better educated, professional classes, attitudes toward marriage do remain conservative among the great majority of American families. But the feeling that a woman is somehow at a disadvantage without a legal marriage no longer exists, at least among America's educated elite.

In short, in America the better educated tend to be the social trendsetters, and it is only a matter of time before their rules spread to the rest of society. Progressive intellectuals were in the vanguard of movements to eliminate racial and sexual discrimination from American society. In general, educated American women have the same pride and self-esteem that characterize only the most outspoken proponents of the women's movement in Japan. In this area, there is an enormous difference between U.S. intellectuals and their counterparts in conservative Japan. Americans with high levels of education tend to be relatively liberal with respect to interracial marriages, homosexuality, and other lifestyle preferences. These ideas are slowly being accepted by the public as a whole, making the United States a much more liberal society, in general, than many other countries. On the other hand, better educated Japanese are much more conservative than their American counterparts, and their ideas have permeated Japan, making it a relatively conservative society.

The granting of independence to teenage children is another area in which Japanese and Americans are very different. America's elite has imitated the custom of the British ruling class in sending its children away from home to prep schools and colleges. Each fall high school students enter America's Ivy League colleges or the prep schools that prepare them for these colleges. These boarding schools perpetuate the traditions of the English "public" school system, providing a rigorous, well-rounded education that inculcates a sense of noblesse oblige. In U.S. society, the higher the family income the greater the likelihood of growing up in a nuclear family and being treated as an independent adult upon reaching the age of eighteen. Such a lifestyle is, of course, associated with freedom and progress. Being independent does not mean that an eighteen-year-old earns his or her own way, however, so the independence a college student enjoys is not independence in the true sense of the word. Prep schools and Ivy League colleges are private schools, the tuitions for which are among the highest in the world. American parents have the thankless role of paying huge sums of money for their children's education without being able to intervene in their daily lives. Perhaps that is one of the burdens of noblesse oblige, but I cannot help feeling that it is also the breeding ground for America's self-centered "me-first" culture.

As a society reaches economic maturity, nonetheless, this is probably the direction it will take. In that sense, although Japan has indeed become rich, compared with the United States, its level of social maturity remains very low. Most Japanese college students live at home with their families, and twenty is the legal age of maturity—the age at which Japanese young people acquire the legal right not only to vote, but to smoke and drink. The whole concept of "independence" is quite different in Japanese society, which from an early age inculcates the importance of a group-centered "we-ism" rather than the self-centered "me-ism" of American society. I suspect that a feeling of disdain for Japan for its perceived social backwardness is implicit in the Japan-is-different argument. An acquaintance of mine who spent a short time in Japan told me that the Japanese she had met (mostly women) were twenty years behind Americans. "They are all pleasure-seeking, living for the moment, absorbed with fashion and material well-being," she complained.

A Shift from the Atlantic to the Pacific? In December 1988, the *Economist* carried an article entitled "America, Asia and Europe: The Pleasures of Three-Part Harmony," which discussed the role of Asia and Japan in American history and speculated about the future. To summarize some of its main points: In 1917, the population of the United States was a hundred million people, 90 percent of whom were whites of European descent. Trade with Europe at that time accounted for 50 percent of America's entire volume of trade. Seventy-two years later, the population of the United States had increased to 250 million people, of whom 75 percent were of European descent, 12 percent were black, 8 percent had emigrated from Latin

America, and 3 percent from Asia.* In that period trade with Europe had dropped to 20 percent of the total, while trade with Asia had jumped to 37 percent. Thus, although Americans of Asian descent accounted for only 3 percent of the total population, 37 percent of America's volume of trade was with Asia.

The proliferating links between America and Asia have caused some to speculate that the United States is shifting away from Europe and toward Asia, as Asia emerges as a force to be reckoned with. In 1988 Joel Kotkin and Yoriko Kishimoto published a book called *The Third Century: America's Resurgence in the Asian Era.* In the first two hundred years of its history, the authors point out, the United States was built by people of European origin, but in America's third century the country's nation-builders will be Americans of Asian descent. Proof for this surmise can be found by examining the activities of Asians in America. Though only 3 percent of the population, Asian-Americans play a significantly larger role in many areas of American life than their actual numbers would suggest. Students of Asian descent make up 25 percent of the student population at UCLA. Approximately 14 percent of the students at Harvard University are of Asian origin. This book concluded that Asia can be expected to play a more forceful role in American life.

Will the Asian era really come about? I have serious doubts on this matter. The fact that Americans of Asian origin account for only 3 percent of the population is not the only problem. First, the rule makers in U.S.

*The figures for minorities in the 1990 census are substantially the same: 2.9 percent for Asian-Pacific Islanders, 12.1 percent for black Americans, and 9 percent for Hispanics.

society are still predominantly Americans of European descent. In the past Asian-Americans have obediently followed these rules, or been forced to follow them. Secondly, there has been little or no visible effort on the part of Americans of Asian descent, especially those of Japanese descent, to make their own rules and to convince the rest of America to accept them as universal values.

Although I have lived in the United States for more than thirty years, I know of no instances when Japanese-Americans, or Japanese nationals working in America, took any action to head off or attempt to resolve today's Japan–U.S. frictions. Every December the topic of Pearl Harbor comes up; it is even dragged in to support current arguments that the Japanese cannot be trusted. Japanese-Americans just listen to these remarks in silence. In America, turning the other cheek is by no means regarded as a virtue. A response such as "Remember Hiroshima and Nagasaki!" or "Apologize for confiscating the property of Japanese-Americans and sending them to internment camps!" would not harm U.S.–Japan relations. On the contrary, the fact that Japanese could argue with impeccable logic on these issues would win them greater respect. Moreover, the United States, unlike Japan, is a country where it is possible for ethnic power to be represented in government. It is both a loss to Japan and a matter for deep regret that Japanese-Americans have initiated no significant political activities on behalf of their country of origin.

Jewish Americans provide the best example of political activism of this kind. Although they account for less than 3 percent of the Americans of European descent,

Jewish Americans have forged a strong link between the United States and Israel. That Israel, with a population of only 4.4 million people, has been able to maintain its independence though surrounded by Arab countries with more than a hundred million inhabitants is due to America's pro-Israel policy and the strong support it receives from the American Jewish community. Jews have a strong ethnic consciousness that has been nurtured both by their religion and by a two-thousand-year history of persecution. Their social and political activism is perfectly compatible with their patriotism as Americans and their love for their ancestral homeland.

Japanese-American soldiers fought against great odds on some of the bloodiest battlegrounds of World War II. They and their families suffered many hardships during the war; many were interned and their property was confiscated. America has now admitted its mistake and paid compensation, but there are other areas in U.S.–Japan relations in which Japanese-Americans can take part. They should emulate their Jewish-American neighbors and speak out boldly to protest American policies that are unfavorable to Asia. The more conspicuous their efforts, the more careful American politicians will be in their words and actions toward Japan. An American politician who made a detrimental remark about Jews would be committing political suicide. Yet Japan-bashing and slurs against Japanese bring in the votes.

America is a country where, in theory, any ethnic group can exercise political power. The majority of U.S. presidents, beginning with George Washington, have been of British ancestry. John F. Kennedy and Ronald

Reagan were two popular presidents of Irish-American origin. Michael Dukakis, who ran against George Bush in the 1988 election, is a Greek-American. Because no one of Greek origin has ever been elected president, wealthy Greek-Americans backed Dukakis whole-heartedly. Although Dukakis was not popular in the South initially and his popularity fell even further during the primaries, he was able to run for president at least partially because of the solid financial support he received from Greek-Americans. Conversely, Richard Gephardt dropped out in the middle of the 1988 campaign because he had no group to put up the money for him.

When I see ethnic power at work, I cannot help feeling chagrined at the weakness and passivity of Asian-Americans, especially Japanese-Americans. Religious Jewish men and boys wear yarmulkes on their heads, proudly calling attention to their difference. Japanese-Americans, on the other hand, try as hard as possible to hide their otherness and blend in. I think these efforts are counterproductive. Of course, Japanese-Americans have their reasons for doing so. During the last world war, after the attack on Pearl Harbor, they experienced discrimination and persecution because of their Japanese background. The memories of how they were suspected of being spies and sent to internment camps are probably still fresh.

Even under wartime conditions, the confiscation of property and forcible internment of noncombatants who hold American citizenship are inexcusable actions. America has formally apologized and paid reparations, but no amount of money can remove the fear Japanese-Americans have that in another crisis Americans will not hesitate to trample on their rights or the rights of any other group of ethnic Americans whose country of origin is at war with the United States. Perhaps this fear has deprived Japanese-Americans of their ethnic and political cohesiveness and made them hesitate to support Japan. If Japanese-Americans were a bit more like Jewish Americans or Italian-Americans, American politicians would be hesitant about attacking Japan. Japan–U.S. frictions might then take a different shape, and many of them, at least, could be averted.

Whatever their personal feelings, Japanese-Americans have not organized to speak out on behalf of Japanese interests. Having devoted themselves entirely to becoming Americans, they are not emotionally oriented toward Japan. In fact, quite the opposite is true. In light of these facts, I cannot agree with the view that America's third century will be an "Asian era." The only way Japanese-Americans seem able to express their loyalty to the United States is by cutting off all ties to their ancestral homeland. Ironically, this absolute and exclusive commitment to a single group is a painfully *Japanese* trait. At best, a single-mindedness, at worst, a parochialism—it has always been both a plus and a minus for Japanese on both sides of the Pacific.

The Indirect Route to Happiness. The article in the *Economist* raises this question: Although clearly the United States has made the shift from Europe to Asia as far as its economy is concerned, have the American people been able to bring their emotional reactions into sync with this change? The answer is clearly "no." As one indication of America's abiding Eurocentricity, the article cites the results of a UNESCO survey of the countries in which American university students had studied in 1985–86. Britain came first with a commanding 29.3 percent; France was next with 13.7 percent; Spain was third with 8.8 percent; Italy and West Germany were fourth and fifth with 7.8 and 6.1 percent, respectively, for a top-five European monopoly. Despite all the talk about economic ties and partnership with Japan, only 2.5 percent of American students abroad went there to study. The rate for China was a mere 1.7 percent, additional proof that Asia is not popular with young Americans. Japan rated even lower than Mexico (4.2 percent) and Israel (4.0 percent). Although the percentage has improved, only 5.1 percent of Americans studying abroad in 1990–91 went to Japan.

Expense, of course, is one factor in determining a student's choice of overseas destination, and language is another. Certainly a common language accounts for much of Britain's popularity with American students. Although the number of students studying Japanese at U.S. universities has been steadily rising from 2.34 percent in 1986 to 3.86 percent in 1990, they still represent only a tiny fraction of the U.S. student population. In short, Americans do not have as much interest in Japan as Japanese think they have, and the country has little appeal to the young people who will be tomorrow's leaders. Foreign study is not sight-seeing; it indicates a commitment to learn something firsthand about the culture of another country. The low percentage of students who are interested in studying in Japan is indicative of the feeling among American students that there is little they want to learn from Japan.

The *Economist* article also presented figures on tourism for 1987. That year 6.2 million Americans went to

Europe, and 4.8 million people from Europe visited the United States. Only 2.3 million Americans traveled to Asia, while 3.3 million Asians came to the United States. These figures tell the story. In comparison with Europe, Asia has limited appeal for Americans even as a tourist destination. Why, despite the deep economic ties, do Americans have so little interest in Asia and especially in an economic superpower like Japan? Why don't students want to study there? The *Economist* article cites "kinship, familiarity and values."

Needless to say, modern civilization originated in the humanistic thought of Western Europe. Most importantly, the concept of "life, liberty, and the pursuit of happiness" is the cornerstone upon which American culture has been built. In Japan, however, there is a long-standing tradition of prizing certain qualities, such as loyalty and honor, even more than life itself. Although the samurai warrior class was abolished more than a hundred years ago, its moral code still lives on in the Japanese people. The Japanese have also traditionally regarded the denial of the self, or selflessness, as a virtue. They attach more importance to the well-being of the whole than to the liberty and happiness of the individual. The pursuit of liberty and happiness on an individual level, therefore, takes low priority.

Japanese are known for suppressing their individual desires for the sake of the group or groups they belong to because they realize that the group is the source of their happiness and security. Once upon a time, the group was the village community or the nation; today it is the corporation. When a Japanese man enters a company, he is supposed to work hard for that company, even at the sacrifice of his immediate personal liberty and happiness. The type of person who, American-style, considers his or her own life and liberty of primary importance is the "nail that sticks out and must be hammered down."

It is easy to understand why Americans feel that the Japanese attitude toward life negates or slights the values that they prize most. Americans look at Japan and see workaholics who spend an hour and a half to two hours a day on packed commuter trains and then work overtime. What is worse, the Japanese do not consume the goods they make but produce them for export. Their income goes straight into savings accounts, the total of which had reached 800 trillion yen in 1992, twice the Gross National Product. They are forced to pay the world's highest prices for rice and beef and cannot buy even a home the size of a "rabbit hutch" because land prices are so absurdly high that the value of metropolitan Tokyo alone is equal to that of the entire United States. Americans accept these stereotypes at face value and conclude that Japanese capitalism has flourished at the cost of human life, liberty, and happiness and is thus clearly different from capitalism in the West.

Attaining something of value can be achieved by different routes, however, and the difference between Americans and Japanese boils down to their respective preferences for "direct" and "indirect" routes. Most Japanese work longer hours than their American or European counterparts, who put in eight hours a day, take a two-day weekend, and have at least two weeks of vacation a year. Most Japanese are willing to work overtime or on holidays if it means better business for their company. At first glance, they seem to be giving up the inalienable human right to liberty. Viewed in a broader context, however, they are simply pursuing their liberty and happiness by indirect means through the intermediary of their corporation.

In Japan an employee of a major company traditionally has not had to worry that he might one day receive a letter from his boss saying that business has gone into a slump and production has to be cut, so he is out of a job. He might have to take a pay cut or work fewer hours, but, as long as he makes no major mistakes in his work, his job is secure. He and his family have access to company welfare and medical services at any time. Company housing may even be available, and though the rooms may be rather small, the rent will be extremely cheap by market standards. The trade-off for larger, more comfortable premises is the savings he can make since he does not have to spend a large portion of his income on rent or upkeep.

The various rewards in life that people in the United States and Europe have to acquire directly by sheer drive and individual effort are often provided to Japanese workers indirectly through the organizations they belong to. A Japanese company may maintain a summer cottage in the mountains or a golf club membership for employee use. Or it may make available at reduced prices tickets to concerts or sports events or even provide the opportunity and the financial means to travel or study abroad. Japan is often described as a company-oriented society, and Japanese employees are known for identifying with their corporations. The reason that corporations have loomed so large in Japanese life is that they are an important medium through which ordinary Japanese have attained happiness in postwar times.

Instead of showing how similar goals can be achieved by totally different means, however, over the last several years the American media have preferred to focus on those aspects of Japan that are most alien and alienating to the American public. At the time of Emperor Hirohito's death in January 1989, for example, American television and newspapers showed Japanese sitting on the ground outside the Imperial Palace overwhelmed by grief. Media reports that these people, or others like them, might commit hara-kiri implied that Japanese feelings toward the emperor are quite different from popular feelings toward the royal families of Europe. Although there were only a few such people, close-ups of them certainly presented a strange sight and helped perpetuate the mistaken impression among Americans watching that this was how all Japanese felt. Because such sights evoke unpleasant memories of the war, they only increase Americans' sense of incompatibility with Japan. In general, the U.S. media tend to be uninformed about Japan, and their sensationalism—if not downright malice—and their utter lack of discretion are obviously harmful to U.S.–Japan relations.

In Japan people seem to be pleased that *kokusaika* (internationalization) has become an English word, but *hara-kiri* and *kamikaze* entered the English language at a much earlier date. Although such words may fade into the background when U.S.–Japan relations run smoothly, when relations are troubled, phrases like "kamikaze businessman" immediately surface. The Japan-is-different argument can all too easily degenerate into a racist slur, a fact that Japanese—and Americans—would do well to remember.

America: Living up to Appearances

Racial Prejudice. As a result of the devaluation of the dollar under the Plaza Accord, America has been reinstated as the world's number one exporter. Germany is second and Japan third. Before the Plaza Accord, West Germany stood first, America second, and Japan third. Thus, although Japan has been criticized worldwide for exporting too much, in fact it trails both the United States and Germany. Why then is Japan singled out for criticism? Why is there no German-bashing?

When I asked American friends about their feelings on this matter, one of them, Professor Richard Zeckhauser of Harvard University, offered some very interesting opinions. There is no Germany-bashing for at least four reasons, he told me. The first is that Germany contributes its share to the international public good. As a member of NATO during the cold war, it made a constructive contribution to world defense, especially to the defense of Europe. Secondly, the German market is thought to be more open than Japan's. Thirdly, German products are not as conspicuous as Japanese goods. Certainly, there are fewer BMWs and Mercedes-Benzes than Japanese cars on U.S. highways, where an American driver will often find a Toyota on the right, a Nissan behind, and a Honda in front. Japanese products also have a more prominent profile because almost all of them are in the consumer electronics field. Although Germany exports a significant number of parts to the

United States, they are hidden within American-made goods and, therefore, are not openly labeled "made in Germany." Consumer goods by their very nature, on the other hand, have to be conspicuous.

Zeckhauser's final point was that the American people understand the Germans. By this he meant that both Germans and Americans are the direct heirs of the Western European cultural tradition. To go even further, both America and Germany belong to the bloc of mature capitalist countries that pursue life, liberty, and happiness. Their brand of capitalism is quite different from that of Japan, where people work too hard, consider business more important than life, and sacrifice their individual liberty and happiness to the interests of their companies.

It would be easy to label this attitude "racial prejudice" as Shintaro Ishihara does; it would also be easy to say, as he did, that "the United States bombed German cities and killed many civilians but did not use atomic bombs on the Germans. U.S. planes dropped them on us because we are Japanese." This sort of statement, however, does not help matters one bit. On the other hand, as even Ishihara acknowledges, "Caucasians created modern civilization." Japan's first order of business should be to give more thought to the concept that lies at the heart of modern Western civilization, that of "life, liberty, and the pursuit of happiness."

American Humanism. America is a far more democratic country than most Japanese realize. Where life, liberty, and the pursuit of happiness are concerned, it is absolutely uncompromising. Japanese frequently complain that the United States has no right to criticize Japan or to meddle in the human rights violations of other countries while doing absolutely nothing about its own problems with drug addiction and homelessness. Americans have by no means ignored the homeless problem, however, as most Japanese seem to think. From a Japanese perspective the situation is clear. If Americans make such a fuss about human rights, why don't they provide for their homeless people so they can live in a manner more befitting human beings? The homeless may not wish to be provided for, however, and under America's thoroughly democratic system, their wishes must be respected.

Manhattan has several shelters that offer clean beds and showers. But when the homeless are taken to such facilities on a bitter cold winter night, someone inevitably complains that the right of the homeless to sleep on the streets or in the parks is being abrogated. In America, even suffering is considered a basic human right if it is a person's choice. The homeless intensely resent being restrained against their will. Anyone foolish enough to propose that the wishes of crazy people should not be respected exposes himself to a blast of criticism from most Americans. City officials must determine how to leave homeless people alone out of respect for their wishes, yet at the same time protect them without incurring the wrath of volunteer organizations and citizens' groups.

In October 1987 New York City began implementing a program to remove mentally ill homeless people from the streets and forcibly provide them with medical and psychiatric care. One of the first people to be picked up and placed in Bellevue Hospital Center was a woman named Joyce Brown. Within a few days Ms. Brown with the help of a lawyer from the New York Civil Liberties Union took legal action against the city. Although her doctors argued that she was a chronic schizophrenic who required medical care, in January, eighty-four days after she had been institutionalized, a judge ordered that she be released.

In front of my house in New York is Washington Square Park, where quite a few homeless people live on a permanent basis. If the temperature drops below freezing, the law allows the city to forcibly put these people in a shelter and keep them there. Because sleeping outdoors when the temperature goes below freezing clearly constitutes a danger to the lives of the homeless, taking them to shelters is not considered a violation of their rights. Under state law, however, a decision by doctors to hold a patient involuntarily for more than sixty days must be approved by a judge. Many doctors complain about the inflexibility of these rules which protect the human rights of those who have mental illnesses—illnesses that could be regulated if they were treated. In Japan such a situation would be regarded as a clear case of taking liberty too far.

Some time ago I buttonholed several American friends and asked them this question: "What do you think about the homeless problem? Don't you think it would be better for the police to forcibly detain the homeless in a clean, comfortable place, even against their wills, to protect their lives?" If I were to ask this question of my Japanese friends, almost certainly all of them would say "yes," but nine out of ten of my American friends said "no." Americans have an almost ab-

normal fear and abhorrence of the exercise of central-
ized power in violation of individual liberties. They are
extremely wary of anything that suggests totalitarian-
ism. Nullifying the rights of the homeless is viewed as
merely the starting point. With that much authority, the
police could easily come to have powers like those of
the Gestapo.

The United States is indeed the champion of the concept of "life, liberty, and the pursuit of happiness." To
an American accustomed to this sort of radical individualism, Japanese-style group consciousness must inevitably seem "different."

The Values of a "Salad Bowl" Society. Japanese think
they have a monopoly on the distinction between ideal
appearances *(tatemae)* and real motives *(honne),* but a
similar distinction exists in America. The difference
between the two countries is that in Japan surface appearances are often attractive but bear little resem-
blance to reality, whereas the United States constantly
tries to live up to its ideals. The most striking example
is America's handling of the racial problem.

The United States is based on the ideal of building a
society free of all discrimination. Progressive American
intellectuals have pushed this ideal to the top of the
country's agenda and made it a national ideology. If
America is a country that has been greatly troubled by
racial problems, it is also the country that has made the
greatest advances in this area. Looking back to the
days when blacks were slaves, when people of color
could not vote or hold important positions in society,
when women and people with disabilities were dis-
criminated against, it is clear how tenaciously America

has adhered in recent decades to the ideal of equality. In reality, of course, American society is still riddled with prejudice, but the United States has made great progress in eradicating discrimination. Japan tends to underestimate the magnitude of America's efforts to live up to its ideals.

During the more than thirty years I have lived in America, I have watched closely and experienced for myself the way Americans have tackled this challenge. When I was thirty-six, I was made a full professor at Brown University, an Ivy League school with a two-hundred-and-fifty-year history. No foreigner of that age could ever hope to be appointed to a full professorship in Japan. In fact, for a long time such an appointment would have been inconceivable in America as well. Despite the reputation the United States now has for scouting out young talent, at one time no Asian, no matter how gifted, could have hoped to attain the position of professor with tenure at a first-rank university. Once the United States decided to eliminate discrimination, however, it made a determined effort to do so.

Many Japanese corporations that have located in the United States have been hit with law suits arising from their treatment of women or their failure to hire African-Americans. These suits are the result of Japanese ignorance about how determined America is to eliminate discrimination. The Japanese know little about the reasons for America's resolute efforts to live up to its ideals. Because the United States is a "salad bowl" composed of many ethnic groups, it cannot function smoothly without a shared system of universal values. Shintaro Ishihara's statement that America dropped the atomic bomb not on Germany but on Japan because of

racial prejudice could only have been made by someone who was unaware of the money and energy the
United States has expended on its racial problem.

Despite America's strenuous efforts to eliminate racism, the Japanese complain that America is prejudiced
against people of color. Prime ministers, cabinet members, and influential members of the Diet have made
statements to that effect. Naturally, these comments
infuriate Americans, especially when these same prime
ministers and cabinet members have made negative
remarks about African-Americans and other ethnic minorities. The United States has officially apologized to
the Japanese-Americans for their internment during
the war and even paid them reparations. Americans
justifiably question the right of Japanese to talk about
discrimination in the United States when Japanese im-
migration laws demand that fingerprints be taken of
any foreigner residing in Japan for more than three
months.

Every nation has taboo subjects that it prefers left
untouched. In America racial prejudice is one such
taboo, a problem Japan has been too ready to discuss.
As I mentioned earlier, in any skillful dealings with
America there is one other button that also must never
be pushed—the one marked national security. These
two issues must be treated with great care. Manhan-
dling either will provoke anger. The book *The Japan
That Can Say "No"* was profoundly guilty in this regard. Part of what it had to say was well thought
of by some Americans, but because it simultaneously
touched on both of these taboo subjects, it angered
many congressmen and, on the grass-roots level, the
members of many minority groups.

Democrats and Republicans were equally enraged by the comments on national security in *The Japan That Can Say "No."* But it was members of the Democratic party, which controls the Congress, who reacted most strongly to the sections on racial prejudice. By antagonizing the entire Congress, the book did tremendous damage to U.S. political strategy vis-à-vis Japan. Before the book appeared, a precarious balance had existed between Congress, which was inclined to attack Japan, and the administration, which tried to smooth over problem areas. But once the pirated edition of the book had been circulated, Congress was given free rein to attack Japan openly. That it is risky to accuse America of racial prejudice is clear.

America sometimes goes too far in the pursuit of its ideals. There is something strange, for example, about telling a university department that it can appoint a professor provided the candidate is black or a woman or a person with a disability. But the employment of visible minorities is a symbol of America's efforts to live up to the ideal of equal opportunity. American universities submit reports to the government detailing how many of their professors are black or women, and funding or financial aid is granted on the basis of these reports. Universities that employ many women and members of minorities, so I've heard, receive government assistance for taking the initiative and putting the country's principles into practice. This is clearly going too far. It is also true, however, that without such efforts, no visible progress would be made.

The Social Security net that the U.S. government generously provides to protect the weak has contributed enormously to the national deficit. America's efforts to help the disadvantaged went too far and under-mined the American economy in the process. That is how far the United States will go to live up to its ideals, and it is foolhardy for Japanese who are unaware of that fact to blithely accuse America of racial prejudice.

FOUR

IN SOME WAYS JAPAN REALLY IS ODD

Manufacturing Is Not the Only Economic Activity

Are Money Games Really Bad? "America has become so engrossed in money games and M&As [mergers and acquisitions] that it no longer makes things. That is why its industrial base has eroded, and the country has gone on a consumer spending spree, buying things from all over the world. This is the basic reason for America's twin deficits. Despite all the talk about service industries and the postindustrial society, it is inevitable that the economy of a country which has forgotten the importance of manufacturing will deteriorate." These observations by Sony chairman Akio Morita are acute. The situation in the United States is almost exactly what he describes. But I would venture to raise two objections. First, is Japan a purely industrial manufacturing country where money games do not exist? Second, are money games really such a bad thing?

Behind the Japanese dislike of money games is a built-in Confucian bias against profiteering or making easy money by manipulating nonproductive assets—buying and selling stocks, companies, or real estate, for example—instead of earning it with the sweat of one's brow. According to this view any money-making activity that is not related to production is the equivalent of gambling. During the 1980s many Japanese viewed the spate of corporate takeovers in the United States with undisguised contempt, as the very phrase *money games* suggests. But if money games are really bad, Japan's land-flipping deals during the late 1980s were probably the worst example of them. With the mere change of a name on a deed of land, the value of a piece of property was inflated by millions or tens of millions of yen. Between 1986 and 1989 speculation in real estate sent the value of land, especially in the metropolitan Tokyo area, soaring to astronomical heights. The price of residential land went up 19.3 percent in 1986 and a whopping 95.8 percent in 1987. For commercial properties the rise was 35.4 percent and 80 percent in those two years. By 1990 the value of land in residential areas was 262.2 percent higher than it had been in 1983; commercial real estate had increased by 312.3 percent in the same period. During the height of the real estate boom a single piece of property might change hands several times at increasingly higher prices. In extreme cases the same piece of land might be sold two or three times in as many months. This must be the most nonproductive money game of them all. If America is to be criticized for its corporate takeovers, then Japan merits the same degree of criticism, or even more, for its real estate deals. In short, Akio Morita told half the truth but neglected to talk about the other half.

The truth is that Japan also regularly engages in nonproductive money games. One would be hard-pressed to argue that land flipping in Japan is good but mergers and acquisitions in America are bad. More to the point, the fact that buying and selling land or companies is a nonproductive practice does not mean such practices have no value. After all, commodities are bought and sold precisely because they do have value. What is regarded as valuable, however, differs from country to country. In America it is companies; in Japan it is land. Japan is about the size of California, but three-quarters of it is mountainous, so the supply of habitable land is severely limited. This makes land extremely valuable, especially in the Tokyo area. America, on the other hand, has a great deal of land; thus, it goes in for mergers and acquisitions, the buying and selling of companies, rather than the buying and selling of land.

If money games are a bad practice, then both Japan and America have been equally guilty of playing them. I do not believe, however, that money games are necessarily bad. At the height of Japan's bubble economy, when Japanese businessmen were asked why the economy was booming, they invariably attributed Japanese prosperity to the high price of land, not to Japan's successful exporting efforts. To put it another way, it was not because the economy was booming that land was in such high demand, but the other way around: Because land was in demand, the economy was booming. People used the vast sums of money they made from land sales on personal consumption or house construction or investments in the stock market or new land purchases, and these transactions boosted the economy. Thus, money games, not making things, were what was behind Japanese prosperity in the late 1980s. In a similar way, what sustained American prosperity during the last decade was the money game known as M&As.

Money games happen as the result of a transfer of ownership. When either land or companies change hands, the economy thrives. From a historical perspective, money games make good sense. Normally, an economy has two sectors, one leading, the other lagging behind. These two sectors change with the times. Nowadays the ultimate nonproductive sector is agriculture. Japanese agriculture is a particularly extreme case, well known for using expensive land to yield insignificant returns. According to the theory of economic development, the decline of agriculture indicates that Japan has made the transition from an agrarian society to a manufacturing society. But until the eighteenth century, agriculture was the most productive sector of all and the source of the world's wealth.

For Japan, too, in the Edo period (1600–1868) the wealth and power of each feudal domain was determined by its *kokudaka,* the amount of rice it produced. The real strength of the clans derived from the agricultural productivity of their fiefs. Even part of their taxes was paid in rice. In the period when agriculture was the mainstay of the productive sector, the nonproductive sectors were the aristocracy, the warrior class, trade, and manufacturing. (This was not manufacturing in the modern sense, of course, but occupations like smithing.) With the Industrial Revolution, however, agriculture declined into a nonproductive sector, and manufacturing emerged as a productive sector. In short, there is a logical progression from the Industrial Revolution to the decline of agriculture and the emergence of the modern state.

As we head into the twenty-first century, however, manufacturing is also ceasing to be a productive sector and is being replaced by knowledge-intensive industries or by service industries. Thus, if the history of the world is a progression from agriculture to manufacturing to knowledge industries, then America's M&As and Japan's land-flipping deals might be thought of as advanced forms of this phenomenon and might even make good economic sense. If the practice of making things, which Akio Morita talked about, has already become a nonproductive sector like agriculture, perhaps both the United States and Japan are risking their futures by trying to hold on to manufacturing jobs. Haven't American and Japanese companies been shifting their manufacturing base to third-world countries where labor is cheap?

This line of thought leads inevitably to the conclusion that money games are the harbingers of the future, the foreshadowings of a postindustrial society that will be the norm for the most advanced countries. That may, in fact, be the case. Heavy physical labor, of which agriculture is an extreme example, overtaxes the body and is the most debilitating kind of work for human beings. The replacement of human labor with machine labor marked the beginning of industrialized society;

today we are perhaps seeing a shift to a knowledge-intensive society that relies chiefly upon human brain power. If that is the case, the fact that we can buy stocks, companies, or land with a single telephone call is completely consistent with the concept of social progress.

That having been said, we will have to consider carefully whether America's M&As and Japan's land-flipping deals were, in fact, the leading edge of such a trend or merely decadent and excessive activities, the symptoms of decline. In making such a judgment, we must look back in time to see whether similar practices have existed in the past. Land speculation in Japan is nothing new; there have been two other land booms in the past twenty or so years alone. The first began in June 1972 when Prime Minister Kakuei Tanaka announced his plan to "remodel the Japanese archipelago" by building high-speed transportation networks to tap the cheap labor supply in the rural areas of Japan. As corporations bought up land along the expected routes, land prices soared, but inflation caused by the upward revaluation of the yen and then the first oil shock in October 1973 sent the Japanese economy into a recession. Tanaka's plans were shelved and many companies found themselves holding land that no one wanted.

The second wave of land speculation occurred ten years later in 1983 and was centered on Tokyo. With the liberalization of the financial and capital markets and Japan's increasing economic importance on the international scene, companies began to flock to Tokyo in the expectation that the city would become a major international center. This trend sent up the cost first of commercial real estate, then of residential areas in Tokyo, and ultimately rippled out into the rest of the country.

M&As and Technological Innovation. M&As are not a new phenomenon either but occur as part of a set cycle. This is the fourth time the United States has witnessed waves of corporate takeovers. The first major wave of mergers and acquisitions in the United States dates back to the late 1890s and lasted through the early 1900s, when today's large corporations such as USX Corporation and Du Pont first began to use corporate takeovers as a means of expansion. During this first wave of M&As, the American economy was in extremely good shape. Because these M&As poured large amounts of previously idle cash into circulation, they inevitably boosted the economy even further. Thus, if M&As are a bad practice, it is because they cause too much of an economic boom and encourage an increase in imports and a consumer spending spree. This phenomenon occurs simply because more money is available—there is nothing wrong with increased market activity per se. An even greater misconception is that the American economy has declined recently because it has been sidetracked by M&As. In fact, it is precisely because M&As were resorted to so frequently that America was able to maintain economic growth and prosperity during the past decade.

America's second wave of M&As came in the 1920s. If the first wave created monopolies, this period saw the creation of oligopolies—the medium-sized companies that make up America's second tier. During this period, too, the economy prospered until the crash of

1929. In American history, a period of merger and acquisition activity is always followed by a crash. The pattern is clear: As long as corporations are being bought and sold, money circulates and creates enormous prosperity, but when the buying and selling comes to an end and the money stops flowing, there is a crash.

The third wave of mergers and acquisitions came during the 1960s and saw the rise of many conglomerates. The keyword during this period was "diversification." The classic example was International Telephone & Telegraph, which ventured out into many different business areas with great success. Up until that time USX only made steel; Ford only made automobiles. But during the third wave of M&As, the concept of the conglomerate took hold. This period of prosperity continued until the first oil shock of the 1970s, and then it too ended in a crash.

The fourth wave occurred in the 1980s. Many of the M&As in that decade served the purpose of corporate restructuring. The bull market of the eighties lasted until the crash of October 19, 1987—"Black Monday"—when Wall Street awakened to the fact that stock prices had gone too high.

As this overview indicates, not only do mergers and acquisitions have a fairly long-standing history in America, they have a set cycle. What is worth noting in this cycle is the cause-and-effect relationship between technology and M&As. Each of the four waves of M&As occurred after some major technological breakthrough had taken place. The first wave in the 1890s occurred after a period of rapid expansion of America's railroad system; prior to the second wave in the 1920s automotive technology had been perfected. The third wave in the 1960s followed the appearance of the jet engine; the fourth wave in the 1980s coincided with the emergence of computer technology.

To understand the causal relation between technology and M&As, let us consider the case of the fourth wave. The introduction of computer technology gave rise to business opportunities that had hitherto been inconceivable. These opportunities accelerated the need for corporate restructuring and led to mergers and acquisitions. Thus, one cannot look only at the M&A phenomenon and dismiss it simply as money games; one must also consider the complex series of trends that have produced it. Mergers and acquisitions do not take place in Japan for the simple reason that a takeover is now considered something that is just not done. (As we shall see in chapter 5, this was not always the case.) An even more significant factor is that few companies ever come up for sale. This is another reason that land, not companies, plays the leading role in Japan's money games.*

Economic Growth Undermines Agriculture. Clearly, both mergers and acquisitions in America and land flipping in Japan were excessive and out of balance. Paradoxically, this very excess is the reason both economies expanded so vigorously in the 1980s. Balanced growth is, in the nature of things, impossible. An econ-

*For a more detailed account of the M&A phenomenon, see "Domestic and International Mergers: Competition or Cooperation" by Ryuzo Sato and Richard Zeckhauser, in *Beyond Trade Friction: U.S.–Japan Economic Relations,* edited by Ryuzo Sato and Julianne Nelson (Cambridge University Press, 1989) pp. 93–120.

omy can grow only when an imbalance occurs. To be sure, the concept of balanced growth does exist in economics, but it designates an ideal state in which all countries, rich and poor, have achieved the same standard of living through economic development. Fortunately, achieving such a state is impossible, since historical trends indicate that imbalanced growth leads to a higher standard of living.

When an economy achieves a balance, stagnation begins to set in. In economics there is a concept called a "product cycle." Take textiles, for example, where the production base has shifted from Europe to America, Japan, and Southeast Asia in search of a low-wage workforce. A country has always been found that is suited to this particular technology. Thus, a product cycle occurs because of technological and economic imbalances among countries. If the world achieved a balance, countries that produce textiles would disappear. To put it another way, water flows because it moves from a higher level to a lower one. Running water produces energy and does not stagnate. In much the same way, imbalances are what energize an economy and keep it running, and a few M&As and land-flipping deals can serve as a priming agent to trigger the economy. As this mode of reasoning suggests, the concept of balanced growth contains two logical contradictions because, first, there is no growth in a balanced state, and, second, growth creates imbalance.

The same point can be explained by what is known in economics as the "price effect" and the "income effect." Suppose there is a product that costs one hundred dollars. Whether this price is considered low or high will depend on a person's income and the current state of his or her pocketbook. Even someone who felt that the item was excessively expensive would buy it if the price were lowered to fifty dollars. This causes the so-called price effect. The same person would also buy if the price did not change but his or her salary suddenly doubled. This is the result of the income effect. The action of buying is ultimately the same, but in the latter case it is clearly justified by an increase in income. What causes an increase in income is economic growth. Economic growth is nothing else but a rise in everyone's income.

But if the economy grows and incomes go up, will everyone be happy? Human nature being what it is, the answer is "not necessarily." An increase in income leads to greater consumption, and when this happens, people start shifting to higher priced goods. This shift is due to what is known in economics as the "elastic income effect." Just such a phenomenon occurred in Japan in the late 1980s. Thanks to the high yen and economic prosperity, Japanese incomes rose steeply. First-class cars on the Shinkansen Bullet Train were full; suddenly young office workers were taking their vacations abroad. Even school trips were to foreign destinations. The world's top brand names sold like hotcakes; indeed, products did not sell very well unless they were expensive. (This is another reason for the difference between Japanese prices and world prices that has led to so much Japan-bashing.)

Japan has certainly become more affluent; it is now the world's largest creditor nation. One might think this is cause for celebration, but, in fact, it is where the idea that "growth creates imbalance" comes into play. When people choose luxury goods, they reject less sophisticated products. This makes the industries that produce such items and the people employed in these industries unhappy. Economic growth, therefore, does not profit everyone in the country; it merely creates new imbalances in the short run.

Statements by Japanese politicians to the effect that both agriculture and automobile manufacturing, mom-and-pop stores and supermarkets will enjoy steady growth are merely political promises and quite incompatible with economic theory. Just as balanced growth for all countries is impossible, balanced growth for all sectors of the same economy is equally impossible. Economic growth creates imbalances and weeds out businesses and entire industries. In Japan, for example, charcoal-making has nearly died out and the charcoal stove has just about disappeared. Young Japanese in their teens and twenties have never known the warmth of coal-heated footwarmers. Most of the textile industry has moved to South Korea, Taiwan, or Hong Kong, or to the member countries of the Association of South-East Asian Nations (ASEAN) or places like Costa Rica.

In the most extreme case, if Japan continues to aim at economic growth and increased income, Japanese agriculture will ultimately be destroyed. With the rise in incomes and the standard of living, the Japanese are no longer consuming as much rice as they used to and are eating bread or meat instead. As the consumption of gourmet food grows, rice consumption will probably drop even further. And as the range of available foods becomes wider, rice will no longer be the main staple of the Japanese diet, but simply a side dish to be eaten in small amounts with steak or fish.

It could be argued that if people really want to eat

rice, it would make better economic sense to buy it cheaply from abroad. The Japanese government's vow not to import a single grain of rice, then, would be only a political gesture aimed at the farming lobby. Were economic development Japan's sole objective this argument would be persuasive because in terms of economic development, Japan's present agricultural policy clearly does not make sense. (In fact, Japanese policies vis-à-vis farming have as much to do with the country's cultural agenda and with preserving the political status quo as they do with economic issues. The Japanese have a great respect for the traditional role of rice farming in Japanese life. On the practical side, farming districts have always been bastions of support for the Liberal Democratic party.) Japan's Staple Food Control Act dates back to 1942 during World War II when the price and distribution of food staples were put under government control with the aim of preventing speculation, maintaining a steady supply, and regulating price fluctuations. Under this system the Japanese government purchases rice and other grains, sets their prices, and controls distribution. Because the government buys rice at a high price from producers and sells it to consumers at a lower price (albeit one far higher than in other countries), the deficit in the food control special account has been growing steadily. The concept of maintaining self-sufficiency in rice became a national security issue in the 1970s. The "food security" argument was first advanced as a reason for blocking the liberalization of rice imports. If Japan were dependent on imports for some or all of its grain supply, the argument goes, food shortages might occur in the event of war.

In short, Japan's basic stance on the rice issue is that rice is a kind of domestic public good. However, rice can also be seen as a private good that can be freely traded. The United States holds the view that rice is just another international trade commodity like cars or consumer electronics and, like other such items, less expensive goods of better quality will naturally prevail in the marketplace. The paradox of Japan's Staple Food Control Law is that under the present system farmers have been protected, but agriculture is being destroyed. For a native of Akita Prefecture such as myself, the beauty of the rice paddies will always be a vivid symbol of my childhood home, one of the major rice-producing centers in Japan. But each time I have gone back to visit in recent years, fewer and fewer of those beautiful, familiar fields remain. Left uncultivated and overrun with weeds, they are a desolate and heart-breaking reminder of the contradiction behind Japanese prosperity. Although everyone talks about protection, rice-growing in Japan is, in fact, bound hand and foot, and the prospects of raising productivity or of making it competitive are fraught with difficulties.

As an economy develops, products that no longer suit society's needs steadily disappear and less productive industries are weeded out. Calling this a "hollowing out" is simply describing the symptoms without trying to understand the phenomenon itself. "Hollowing out" is actually a normal state of economic development, proof that the economy is operating efficiently. If an industry in one country "hollows out," some other country that can fill the resulting niche will get rich in the process. The history of economic development has consisted of a succession of "hollowing out" processes.

Manufacturing eroded agriculture because it was more productive than farming. Similarly, the productivity of the knowledge industries is superior to that of manufacturing so the erosion of manufacturing is only natural. That is the law of economic development.

What Causes the Disparity between Japan's Prices and World Prices?

The Plaza Accord Fiasco. By the end of the 1980s America had become extremely nervous about Japanese investments in U.S. real estate. In particular, the purchase of Rockefeller Center provoked a strong backlash. How could such a sale take place? The remote cause can be traced back to the Plaza Accord in 1985. The yen had started to appreciate in February 1985, and in one sense the actions taken by the finance ministers and central bankers of the five major industrial powers at the Plaza Hotel in September of that year simply confirmed the fundamental forces at work in the marketplace. There is no denying, however, that then Secretary of the Treasury Jim Baker believed that helping this trend along and lowering the value of the dollar would make American goods more competitive. This was a total miscalculation on the part of the Reagan administration, as America has come to realize. Between 1985 and 1988, the value of the dollar dropped from 240 yen to the 120-yen level. Although it later gradually rose again to around 150 yen, in September 1992 it fell below 120 yen for the first time in postwar history.

The cheap dollar policy embodied in the Plaza Accord was supposed to solve America's trade deficit and open the Japanese market to U.S. goods. The American projection was that an upward revaluation of the yen would lead to a reduction in Japan's exports and thus in its trade surplus with the United States. In due course Japan would be forced to open its markets. This did not happen. Instead, in an amazingly short time Japan had overcome the adverse effects of the high yen and strengthened its economy even further. Moreover, thanks to the high yen, Japan's income doubled in the space of a mere four or five years. The U.S. government had not dreamed this would happen; nor had it imagined that Japan would set about "buying America" with its newly doubled income. In effect, the Plaza Accord cut the value of America in half and made Japan twice as rich as it previously had been. It was a colossal mistake.

For a million yen to double in value in ten years' time, it would have to be invested at an interest rate of 7 percent compounded annually. To double in four years would require an interest rate of 15 or 16 percent. In other words, the United States gave Japan an annual growth rate of 15 to 16 percent free of charge. Anyone with even a nodding acquaintance with economics can understand how huge these figures are. Moreover, as a side effect, it contributed to the discrepancy between the price of goods in Japan and what these same items sell for abroad.

The price gap problem is two-sided. On the one hand, Japanese goods are expensive at home and inexpensive abroad; on the other hand, foreign goods suddenly become absurdly expensive when they arrive in Japan. There are two reasons for this. First, price adjustments do not keep up with rapid fluctuations in the exchange rate. The second source of the problem is Japan's economic structure, which has become the target of anti-Japanese attacks.

Given the continuing cheap-dollar, high-yen exchange rates, it is odd that Japanese exports have not become more expensive in the United States and that U.S. exports have not gotten much cheaper in Japan, if not in the same proportion as the exchange rate, then certainly by a considerable degree. This has not occurred. The advantages of the cheap dollar have not been passed on to American producers any more than the advantages of the high yen have been passed on to consumers in Japan.

In Japan the failure to pass along the benefits of the high yen can be laid at the door of two groups. Half of the responsibility lies with the buyers, the Japanese people themselves. Responsibility for the other half, of course, lies with the suppliers and sellers. As incomes rise, consumers are quite willing to buy expensive items; there is even a tendency, which might be regarded as a Japanese trait, to buy things precisely because they are expensive. That makes it difficult for businesses to lower their prices. The cost of materials even for luxury items is often not very great, but many Japanese feel that the more costly an item is the better it must be. That is why Japanese buy 80 percent of the brand name items produced by Gucci and Louis Vuitton, items that are ridiculously expensive. Diamonds also sell because they are expensive; if they were cheap, no one would be interested in buying them. In short, the Veblenesque price effect operates for expensive goods. On the other hand, suppliers make good use of Japan's complicated distribution system by taking advantage of the sole agency dealership system, which gives the supplier monopoly rights over the goods sold in a particular store. The distribution problem is indeed structural.

No one can explain fully, however, why it is cheaper to buy Japanese goods overseas than in Japan. Although, as we saw in chapter 1, technological innovation and economies of scale account in part for why price increases have been held to a minimum regardless of the high yen or the low dollar, no completely satisfactory explanation has been proposed as to why Japanese goods cost less abroad than they do at home. The Japan External Trade Organization (JETRO) has argued that the high cost of land, especially in Tokyo, contributes to the price gap by increasing overhead for small retailers which is then passed on to customers in the form of higher prices. By postulating what is known in economics as "price discrimination," one could explain why goods for export are cheap and those for domestic use are expensive, but this would be a clear case of dumping and a problem of corporate morality rather than a structural issue. In short, there is no simple economic explanation for this aspect of the price gap. Though by no means all, many products that are made in Japan are in fact cheaper in the United States. During the Structural Impediments Initiative talks the American side confronted Japan with a list of them. Cameras are a prime example. The president of a Japanese camera-making company is said to have come to America just to buy his own company's cameras because they were cheaper here. A former prime minister, while on a state visit, is rumored to have bought a Japanese camera at a famous New York discount store. These stories and others too numerous to mention indicate popular Japanese perceptions of the problem.

The explanation America gives for the price gap is interesting: The reason Japanese goods can be bought more cheaply in America than in Japan is that America has an extremely efficient distribution system. Conversely, the reason American goods and even Japanese goods are more expensive in Japan is that the Japanese distribution system is extremely inefficient. Whether this observation is correct or not, it is an open secret that Japan's distribution mechanism is so complex that it has been called the "Dark Continent." Reform of the Japanese distribution system was near the top of the agenda during the U.S.–Japan Structural Initiative Impediment talks.

The Japanese market is characterized by a high density of very small outlets and a multilayered wholesale system. According to a recent Japanese government white paper put out by the Economic Planning Agency, 93 percent of all small retail stores in Japan had fewer than ten employees, and there were 135 stores for every 10,000 people. In contrast, the United States had only 81 stores per 10,000 people and Germany only 67.

How can we account for the large number of small stores in Japan? The answer to that question can be found in consumer habits and cultural background. The average family in Japan consumes more fresh produce than its American counterpart and shows a strong resistance to frozen foods. Furthermore, few homes have a large storage capacity. This means that the average Japanese housewife shops on a daily rather than a weekly basis, and stores are more likely to be within walking distance of her home. Yet another reason is that Japanese consider shopping as a form of entertainment, and a store often serves as a kind of meeting place. The Yaohan Supermarket in Fort Lee, New Jersey, is a good example of how these Japanese concepts have been imported to America and incorporated into the store's design. In addition to shopping facilities, the supermarket contains restaurants where mothers with small children can put down their parcels and relax, have a meal and talk to friends and acquaintances. Taking the family to a department store on the weekends is a typically Japanese idea of shopping as a form of entertainment.

Another reason for the high density of small outlets in Japan is said to date back to the occupation. There is a story—perhaps apocryphal—that when General MacArthur was compiling a report on reconstruction efforts in Japan to submit to the U.S. government, the unemployment figures at the time were unexpectedly high—nearly 40 percent. Because this would reflect badly on the soundness of occupation policy, it was decided that anyone who was living with an employee of one of the many small retail stores throughout Japan would not be counted as unemployed, even if, in fact, they were. This strategy reduced the unemployment rate to 20 percent. In short, because most of the small retail outlets in Japan were—and still are—family-run mom-and-pop stores, the statistics were manipulated to conceal unemployment within families. This sort of manipulation continues to the present day and must be taken into consideration in accounting for Japan's extremely low unemployment rate.

Shopping districts composed of dozens of these tiny stores all crowded together have traditionally played an important role in the local economy and have contributed much to the character of local society. The Large-Store Law was enacted in 1973 to prevent large supermarkets, which had just begun to move into these districts, from adversely affecting the small retailers who had been there for years. In effect the law allows the local chamber of commerce to decide whether any changes need to be made to the size, operating hours, and other plans for a proposed large store. As a result of the Structural Impediments Initiative talks, amendments to the Large-Store Law and related legislation were proposed, including shortening the deliberation process from a year and a half to a year and increasing to a hundred square meters the area in large stores where foreign imports could be sold. The American retailer Toys 'R Us has succeeded in setting up outlets, and large Japanese supermarkets have begun to follow suit.

The multilayered structure of the wholesale system can be viewed as a necessary result of the need to supply this extremely large number of retail stores efficiently and often. Consumers in Japan are said to be the most demanding in the world, and in recent years their needs have diversified considerably. Although diversification would seem to promote a multilayered structure, this argument is counterbalanced by the rapid growth of convenience stores which are absorbing many of the smaller stores in their vicinity. On the Izu peninsula south of Tokyo, where I spend several months of the year, I can see this phenomenon happening right in my own neighborhood: The small stores are being rapidly forced out of business by a big new supermarket. In any event, it is fair to assume that the distribution sector in Japan faces a major shake-up.

The Price Gap as Proof That Japan Is Different. Is there a way to eliminate the discrepancy between Japanese and international prices for the same goods? Theoretically, yes. If a different exchange rate were adopted for each product, then the gap would soon disappear.

Broadly speaking, the exchange rate is determined by two factors. The first is the flow of trade between the United States and Japan, that is, the supply and demand for the goods actually being traded between the two countries—beef and oranges, VCRs and automobiles. If the demand for Japanese goods is heavy in America, the dollar goes down; if the demand for American goods is heavy in Japan, the dollar goes up.

The second factor is the flow of capital. When Mitsubishi bought Rockefeller Center, it could not make the purchase in yen so it sold yen on the exchange market and bought dollars to pay for the landmark property. Having purchased Rockefeller Center, Mitsubishi, of course, could not actually take it back home to Japan. What Mitsubishi received was not the asset itself but a piece of paper, the title to the property. Similarly, Japan often purchases U.S. bonds. Yen are exchanged for dollars on the exchange market, and these dollars are used to buy pieces of paper, bonds, which are taken back to Japan. This trade in assets, rather than things, is called the flow of capital. When Japan set about "buying America," it inevitably exchanged yen for dollars so the demand for dollars increased and the value of the dollar went up. Conversely, in the past two years when Japan lost interest in the United States and withdrew its money, it sold dollars and bought yen, and the dollar declined. Thus, the exchange rate is determined by the flow of both goods and capital.

To understand how adopting a different exchange rate for each product would eliminate the price gap, consider land in Japan, the price for which is very high. The Imperial Palace occupies a large site in the center of Tokyo and is, of course, the prime piece of real estate in Japan. But when the book value for that single piece of property could buy the entire country of Canada—as it could in the late 1980s—something is very wrong.

The value of the Imperial Palace was so incredibly high because the dollar was then trading at around 150 yen. Suppose, however, that one dollar had been worth 1,500 yen; Japanese land would have immediately dropped to one tenth its value. If the rate of 1,500 yen to the dollar had been adopted only for land transactions, the criticism implicit in comments about how Japan's high land prices were keeping out foreign companies would have vanished in a flash.

In the 1980s airfares in Japan were also expensive so the exchange rate for them should have been around 500 yen to the dollar. Conversely, electronic appliances were cheap so the exchange rate for them could have been set at 110 yen to the dollar; and the one for cars might have been 100 yen. Establishing a different exchange rate for each item would not only eliminate the price gap but would simultaneously solve the trade surplus/deficit problem. Such a move would satisfy U.S. demands to make things "just like they are in America." The problem with this method is that it might lead to cheating. Suppose, for example, someone claimed he was planning to buy land in Japan and received the real estate exchange rate of 1,500 yen to the dollar. If he then turned around and used this favorable exchange rate to purchase a car with an exchange rate valued at 100 yen to the dollar, such cheating would ultimately corrupt the conversion system.

The reason I have proposed such a fantastic hypothesis as multiple exchange rates that vary with different goods is that ideally the exchange rate system ought to prevent discrepancies in the value of a particular commodity from occurring between countries. Only in Japan, however, do we encounter the strange situation that a balance between its prices and those of the rest of the industrialized world cannot be achieved unless the exchange rate for land is 1,500 yen to the dollar and the one for automobiles is 100 yen to the dollar. This fact by itself bears witness to the fundamental difference in the economic fabrics of the United States and Japan. From an international perspective, Japan is an enormously unbalanced country.

In general, this strange situation does not exist between Europe and the United States. In the late eighties, the German currency, like the yen, nearly doubled in value, but this did not produce the same imbalances in western Germany that it did in Japan. The German economy has a mechanism to correct any imbalances created by fluctuations in the exchange rate. Of course, a price gap for some items does exist between Germany and the United States, but nothing as extreme as in Japan, where land is worth much more than in America, but cars are only worth a fraction as much.

If we keep in mind what constitutes fair prices in the

international marketplace and try to coordinate them by setting a different hypothetical exchange rate for each item, it becomes perfectly clear, even to Japanese eyes, how unbalanced Japanese prices are compared with prices in Europe and North America. Japanese may retort that as long as they have the money and can find someone willing to sell to them, it does not matter if Japan as a country contains these imbalances whatever the rest of the world might think. To American and European eyes, however, these imbalances reflect what makes Japan "different." If, for example, the appropriate exchange rate for cars in Japan is 100 yen to the dollar and the exchange rate is adjusted accordingly, then existing prices for cars are too low. Similarly, if a fair exchange rate for land is 1,500 yen to the dollar, then existing Japanese land prices are too high.

According to the rules of capitalism, no one will buy land that is too expensive, whereas cheap cars sell briskly. Items that do not sell eventually come down in price, and the prices for things that do sell go up, thereby achieving a balance. This is what is known as a market mechanism. In Japan, however, market mechanisms do not work. According to Americans and Europeans, they do not work because Japan is different. That was the lesson they learned from the Plaza Accord fiasco. At the time, the finance ministers and central bankers of the United States, Japan, West Germany, Great Britain, and France believed that adjusting the exchange rates would remedy Japan's chronic trade surpluses and bring the Japanese economy more into line with economic conditions in Europe and North America. In other words, the Plaza Accord was based on the presupposition that Japan's economic structure was *not* different from that of the rest of the industrialized world. But, in fact, this was not the case. Not only did the Plaza Accord fail to improve the chronic surplus, it created a price gap between Japanese and international prices that even market mechanisms failed to eliminate. Japanese capitalism, the Western world has come to believe, is so different that adjusting exchange rates has no effect at all.

Emotional Borders in a Borderless Age

Ominous Signs from America's Grass Roots. With the failure of the Plaza Accord, a view began to emerge in America that exchange rates should be determined not just by the flow of trade and capital but also on the basis of PPP—purchasing power parity. Purchasing power parity is a method of determining the exchange rate in terms of the true cost of living in any two given countries. In Japan and the United States, for example, one would take the price of land, the price of automobiles, and so forth, and come up with an average by which to determine what the exchange rate should be. But for PPP to function properly two conditions are necessary. The first is that the productivity and technological skills of the two countries being compared must be roughly on the same level. Second, consumer tastes must also be roughly equivalent.

When these two conditions are present, using PPP to determine the exchange rate works perfectly. The reason the exchange rates between America and Europe are in agreement is that there are no major differences in technological skills, and tastes are remarkably similar. The exchange rates between the United States and the countries of Europe are actually determined by the balance in supply and demand of capital and trade goods, but if the rates were determined by PPP, there would be little or no change. In contrast, the exchange rate between the United States and Japan inevitably produces a gap between Japanese and U.S. prices. This gap is caused by the fact that Japanese society and American society really are different. In the Japanese economic system, for example, there is no "invisible hand" at work to eliminate the spread between domestic and international prices. And even if no difference in technological skills existed, the two countries' tastes are different. An extreme example of the differences in Japanese and American tastes is their attitudes toward *natto.* Natto is a kind of fermented bean dish that most Japanese are extremely fond of, but of all the Americans I know who claim to like Japanese food because it is low in fat and low in calories, I have never met anyone who likes natto very much. Because such an extreme difference in tastes inevitably affects the price of a product, it is only natural that natto is more expensive in the United States than it is in Japan. This is a price gap that it would be difficult even for the "invisible hand" to eliminate.

The very fact that tastes differ is evidence of a deeper difference. If tastes are different, each country's emotional response to a product is different, and this difference in emotional response will naturally affect the product's price. I once had a conversation with the Saudi Arabian ambassador to Japan. Noticing that he carried a lot of keys, I asked him why he had so many. One was the key to the house, he explained, another was the key to his office, and another was the key to the television. Surprised by this answer, I asked why he needed a key to the television. "So my children can't watch it," he replied. Saudi Arabia has strict religious rules against the depiction of naked women. Thus, the ambassador could not allow his children to look at Japanese television, which features a great deal of violence and pornography.

In short, when tastes differ, people approach the same product in different ways. I do not know how much television sets cost in Saudi Arabia, whether they are more or less expensive than they are in the United States or Japan. What is certain, at any rate, is that the attitudes toward television which prevail in America and Japan do not prevail in Saudi Arabia. Even the exchange rate is virtually powerless in the face of taste. Differences in prices for the same product between one culture and another are probably inevitable. Or to put it the other way around, the role played by culture and taste is very important.

These differences in culture and taste played a large part in the rise of revisionism discussed in chapter 1. Revisionists took note of them to develop the argument that Japan is different. What lent credence to the revisionists' point of view is that adjustments to the exchange rate did not diminish Japan's trade surplus with the United States but only succeeded in creating a price gap between the two countries. A trade balance was achieved with Europe and even with Germany, which was affected by an upward revaluation of the mark at more or less the same rate as the yen. To the question why a trade balance has not been reached with Japan alone, the revisionists' answer that "Japan is different" carried conviction. Looked at from another perspective, the fact that a trade balance has not been reached is testimony to Japan's strength. It demonstrates Japan's ability to transform an unfavorable set of circumstances into a favorable one. This is the theory of comparative disadvantage. A person with a disability, for example, must learn to compensate for and overcome his or her personal handicap in order to survive. Japan's handicap is a shortage of land, which it must utilize to its highest potential if it hopes to be competitive with other countries in trade. External forces have compelled the Japanese to work more diligently than others in order to remain competitive. Hence Japan has turned a disadvantage—its limited land area—into an advantage.

Aggressive Japanese investment in the United States during the late 1980s, however, has rubbed Americans' feelings the wrong way. The people responsible for selling Columbia Pictures and Rockefeller Center may have walked away from those deals with big smiles on their faces, but Americans are uncomfortable that foreigners now own these institutions which embody so much of the American tradition that they had almost come to be regarded as public property. In fact, of course, Rockefeller Center is merely a large piece of real estate and Columbia Pictures was just another troubled business. It is not a healthy situation, however, when the American media and ordinary Americans use the sale of these properties to make a fuss about the financial presence of Japan in the United States. If America's grass roots come to believe that Japan aims at the economic domination of the world—though it in fact has no such aims—matters will be complicated considerably. There are many American companies such as Motorola that are getting rich by accommodating themselves to the differences between Japan and America. Companies that are doing well, however, do not speak out; the companies that complain are always the ones that are doing poorly.

Generally speaking, American companies have far less official clout than their Japanese counterparts and not nearly as much power to affect government decisions. The American public is quite a different story. Once aroused it can move mountains.

Distorted Nationalism. Although Japanese investment in America fell from $16 billion a year in 1988–90 to $5 billion a year in 1991, if a representative sampling of Americans were asked what they thought about Japanese investment in America, I suspect a large majority would still answer that it is a bad thing. The mass media has overplayed the issue and focused only on the facts that portray Japan in a negative light. Americans who read biased articles or see sensationalized reports on television become convinced that these accounts are accurate. And once the politicians join in and begin Japan-bashing, a great chorus of "Japan is unfair" goes up throughout America.

This is what I call my "hospital patient" argument. If someone is in the hospital, something must be wrong with him. If you ask several patients if anything is wrong with them, you can be sure they will all answer "yes." But if, based on this partial survey, you report that most of the people in the world are sick, that is obviously incorrect. The American mass media frequently resort to this sort of trick. Strictly speaking, *The*

Japan That Can Say "No" expressed the views of only two people, but the book was portrayed as an expression of the views of the Japanese people as a whole. This is distorted nationalism, and nationalism in one country gives rise to nationalism in the other.

Nationalism plainly resides in the human heart. At the time of the FSX hearings, I was perplexed at America's behavior, which seemed only a pretext for getting its own way. The reason for my reaction was, quite simply, that I am Japanese. When I visited Japan still angry about the incident and discussed it with the then chairman of Mitsubishi Heavy Industries, he was calm and collected. "Don't get so excited," he told me, "it's only business." Perhaps a businessman's heart is an uncongenial place for nationalism to reside; perhaps he only has room in his heart for business. The American business world is just the same. If an American asked Rockefeller what he thought he was doing selling Rockefeller Center, he would undoubtedly say, "Don't get so upset. I've just made an extremely good deal with Japan."

In fact, both Mitsubishi Estate Company and Rockefeller were very concerned about the American public's reaction and held repeated discussions about how to announce the deal. Just as they feared, the announcement created an uproar. The American media, who had nothing directly to do with Rockefeller, caused a stir that reverberated throughout the country. The same thing happens in Japan. When an American company is bought by a Japanese company, Japanese newspapers report the takeover as though it were a natural and normal activity. What happens when the shoe is on the other foot, however? When T. Boone

Pickens acquired a mere 26 percent in the Koito Manufacturing Company, the Japanese mass media treated
the incident as a matter for grave concern.

By American standards of common sense, it is perfectly reasonable for someone holding 26 percent of a
company's stock to ask to be on the board of directors.
In fact, Toyota, which holds only a 19 percent share in
Koito, has three representatives on the board. Logically, Pickens should have had at least the same number of board members as Toyota. But Koito refused
Pickens's request for a single seat on the grounds that
he is a "greenmailer" who has a bad reputation in the
United States. Emotional issues aside, this decision was
totally irrational from an economic standpoint.

When stocks are offered for public sale, no one is in
a position to dictate how many any one individual buys.
Those who buy in large quantities become major stockholders, and it is natural that they should have a say in
management. Because there is no law that prevents
people with bad reputations from buying stocks, Pickens's request was absolutely legitimate. That may be
unsettling to the company whose stock he bought, but
it makes perfectly good economic sense.

Pickens ultimately gave up, but during his two-year
fight for a seat on Koito's board, he encouraged U.S.
authorities to investigate other exclusionary Japanese
business practices on the grounds that they might be
monopolistic or involve other illegalities such as collu-
sion. His own dealings, however, left many questions
unanswered. The *New York Times* on May 5, 1991, reported that Pickens had "bought the stock from a Japanese entrepreneur who, after failing to get Toyota to
buy it at a premium, took it to Mr. Pickens in hopes that

an international incident would arise. He also lent him the money to buy the shares, apparently guaranteeing him against risk.... So every time Mr. Pickens demanded that Toyota come clean, the Japanese demanded that he do the same."

Even though economic borders may now in fact be next to nonexistent, emotional borders, in the form of resistance and opposition to international mergers and acquisitions within both Japan and the United States, are growing even stronger. Despite the grumbling on the American side, the flow of money and goods between the United States and Japan is already fairly free. But when people enter the equation, they are regarded as "intruders," as in the Pickens affair, and touch off Japanese defense mechanisms. America's instinctive defensive reaction against Mitsubishi was another instance of an emotional border.

Furthermore, the people who actually benefit from these transactions in most cases are not the foreign companies that provoked the defensive reaction. In the Koito case, the unidentified Japanese entrepreneur behind Pickens did not become an issue; nor did Rockefeller come in for any criticism when he profited from the sale of Rockefeller Center. Instead, Mitsubishi Estate Company was accused of stealing an American landmark. The economic frictions between the United States and Japan that have become prominent recently teach us that, regardless of whether our economies are borderless or not, the emotional borders that divide one country from another are as firmly in place as ever.

Today the phrase "borderless economy" is quite common. To be sure, the flow of people, things, and money ignores national borders. But one border still remains, the border that exists in people's hearts. No matter how much progress is made in creating a global economy, I suspect people will continue to harbor nationalist sentiments to the very end. After so much Japan-bashing, many Japanese, I am sure, heartily agreed with Shintaro Ishihara's statements. A proportional number of Americans were probably equally annoyed when they read his book.

Until recently I used to think that these emotional borders should be dismantled as soon as possible. But living as I do in American society which, more than fifty years after Pearl Harbor, has still not overcome its wariness of Japan, I am now more inclined to be realistic. Emotional borders in the form of nationalism and chauvinism will always be with us; the heart is one area that can never become completely borderless. Since there is no point in holding up unrealistic, unattainable ideals, let us make honest efforts to see to it that, in the problem areas that remain, we do not make political issues out of these emotional barriers.

FIVE

IS A PAX JAPONICA POSSIBLE?

The "Amerippon" Concept

Conditions for Leadership. Paul Kennedy's *The Rise and Fall of the Great Powers* was highly acclaimed in Japan because it contains two messages that are welcome to Japanese ears. The first is that the age of the great power (America) is coming to an end. The other is that the age of Japan is about to begin. But the Japanese have interpreted Kennedy's work in a much too subjective fashion. Furthermore, references to Japan can only be found on a dozen or so pages of this very thick tome.

Most Japanese readers bought this hefty history book to read those pages. Even the book's author readily acknowledges this fact. In 1988 I was asked by a Japanese magazine to interview Kennedy, and two or three days before he was to go to Japan, I talked with him for a few hours in his office at Yale University. Primarily a military historian, Kennedy is a recognized authority in his field. He expressed surprise at the response *The Rise and Fall of the Great Powers* had received in Japan, though he noted with some regret that the only section most of his Japanese readers seemed to have read was the one in which he predicted that America will decline and Japan or some other country will come to the fore.

I must take issue with Kennedy in two areas. First, he cites America's enormous defense expenditures as one of the reasons the country has declined. U.S. defense spending, however, is roughly 5 or 6 percent of the GNP, hardly enough to account for America's decline. His argument seems even less relevant as we enter the post-cold war era and face the transitional problem of moving resources from the defense industry to nondefense industries, thereby incurring a "peace penalty" resulting from the difficult reallocation of resources. Kennedy may be an eminent historian, but his discussion of economic issues is somewhat amateurish. A more important factor in America's decline, I think, is that the conditions for great power status—competitiveness, culture, and the very principles of nationhood—are giving way. In a competitive world, it is natural for the country holding the dominant, monopolistic position to feel secure and relaxed, thus slowly losing its competitive edge. Other countries use the dominant country as a target to be overcome, thus increasing their competitiveness and eventually overtaking their stagnant target. As a result, America is beginning to find it difficult to maintain its edge.

The other problem area is Kennedy's lack of firsthand knowledge about Japan. When I visited him in 1988, he was about to make his first visit there. The ideas about Japan that he expresses in *The Rise and Fall of the Great Powers* are strictly secondhand. Possibly that is why he seems to think that in the future both Japan and China will become number one—he lumps the two countries together. I find this totally incomprehensible. Kennedy's rationale seems to be that China is a vast country with a three- or four-thousand-year history. Egypt and India are also civilizations with four- or five-thousand-year histories, but that does not mean they can become future superpowers. The thought often occurs to me that, with some exceptions, Americans who have had no actual experience of living in the Far East are China fans. Perhaps because Americans of Chinese descent make up the largest part of the Asian community in the United States, Americans tend to associate all Asians with China and not distinguish between people from different Asian nations.

In short, Kennedy's predictions have no solid historical foundations. They are only a matter of feelings. And because these feelings are pleasing to Japanese sensibilities, his book was very popular in Japan. For a short time Kennedy was lionized by the Japanese mass media, which hung on his words as though he were some kind of oracle. *The Rise and Fall of the Great Powers* also sold well in the United States, but many intellectuals were critical of the book. One of the first to criticize it was Harvard political scientist Joseph Nye, who in 1990 published a book entitled *Bound to Lead: The Changing Nature of American Power,* which refuted the fundamental assumptions of *The Rise and Fall of the Great Powers.*

Another critic was Zbigniew Brzezinski. The assistant to the president for national security affairs during the Carter administration, Brzezinski is the author of *The Grand Failure,* which was also much talked about in Japan when it came out in 1985. In that book Brzezinski had accurately predicted that the fall of communism was more likely than an American decline. At the request of a Japanese newspaper I had a discussion with Brzezinski in January 1990. When I asked him what he thought of the Kennedy book, he replied that it is completely wrong. As a history book—that is, as an account of the past—it is excellent, but when Kennedy attempts to predict the future, his argument becomes quite faulty. When I asked him who would lead the world ten or twenty years from now, his reply was "America, of course." In other words, there will be no Pax Japonica.

Brzezinski is not a member of the Chrysanthemum Club, but he has studied Japan closely and has even published a book on the subject. While he would not claim to be an authority on Japan, he lived there for a year on a Rockefeller Foundation fellowship and knows the country far better than many self-proclaimed experts. At the very least, the fact that his book, *The Fragile Blossom,* is not based simply on abstract ideas is commendable.

To my question whether Japanese leadership of the Asia-Pacific region is inconceivable, Brzezinski answered that it probably is. There are many conditions for leadership, he explained. Economic strength is one; population is another. No matter how strong Israel is, for example, it can never achieve world leadership. Even if there were ten fewer Arabs for every Israeli, the Israelis would still be outnumbered. Next, when all is said and done, military power is needed to protect economic power. And, finally, leadership cannot come

about without a culture or an ideology capable of leading the world. If Brzezinski had added one more item,
religion, to his four conditions for leadership, the list
would probably be complete.

How many of these conditions does Japan satisfy? In
truth, all it has at present are economic power and a
population of 120 million people. Japan certainly has
its own religion, ideology, and culture, but these do
not have the universal appeal of "life, liberty, and the
pursuit of happiness." For Japan to become the world's
leader, it is commonly conceded, is probably impossible. As mentioned earlier, leadership is not determined
by consensus or mutual agreement. In a manner of
speaking, a master-servant relationship exists in international relations. Moreover, history teaches that war
has always preceded a change in leadership. The wars
between Spain and Portugal in the sixteenth century
and between England and Holland in the seventeenth
century are good examples. If Japan tried to seize leadership without a war, other countries would be unlikely
to align themselves with Japan unless it had a universal system of values or a universal appeal. Brzezinski
illustrated this fact most pointedly when he asked how
many countries in Asia would follow Japan. When Japan's military expenditures went over their meager
limit of 1 percent of GNP, China, Korea, and Singapore
all protested that Japan was rearming. The Japanese
cannot assume leadership without military power, but
Japanese military power is what other Asians fear
most. It is impossible for Asia to call Japan "leader."

I believe Brzezinski's analysis is probably correct. A
country, like a person, must have leadership qualities,

and it must be popular among the countries that it hopes to lead. Unfortunately, the people of the world do not much like today's Japan.

Are the Basic Assumptions in The Rise and Fall of the Great Powers *Correct?* In the course of our conversation, Brzezinski also suggested that Japan put its great economic strength to good use internationally and globally. As a specific measure, he proposed the concept of "Amerippon"—that the United States and Japan should combine their strengths to influence the future course of the world.

What Brzezinski was saying is that America and Japan must find a way to join forces. Such an arrangement would make for smooth going in a number of areas. For example, America is more trusted in Asia than Japan is. Thus, negotiations there would go far more smoothly if America were in the foreground and Japan followed along behind than if Japan acted on its own. It is likely that only through such an arrangement—Amerippon—will Japan be able to gain a foothold in Asia and be respected.

A "Pax Japonica" certainly sounds more pleasing to the Japanese. It has a nice ring to it. In the 1980s before the collapse of Japan's bubble economy and the succession of political scandals, some people believed that, just as the transition from the Pax Britannica to the Pax Americana involved a shift in power from one side of the Atlantic Ocean to the other, a similar shift from one side of the Pacific to the other was about to occur. Just as world trends moved from Yalta to Malta, this argument went, they were now moving in the direction of disarmament and a "peace dividend." Soon the age of military power would be over, and a new age of economic power would dawn. *Perestroika,* the rise of democracy in Eastern Europe, the collapse of the Berlin Wall, the dissolution of the Soviet Union, all made an opening for economic power. And economic power means Japan.

The Pax Japonica is a dangerous seduction, an unattainable dream, an illusion. In the past, world leadership has only changed hands after a victory in war. In the future this may not hold true, but it has been the case up until now. The present-day rationale behind military might among the major world powers is no longer its use for territorial expansion or to invade other countries but to protect one's own economic interests. The logical conclusion to be drawn from this is: If Japan is truly aiming for world leadership, it must arm itself to protect both its supply line for essential energy resources and the assets it has invested in throughout the world. Then, even if a revolution like the one in Iran occurs, Japan would not simply shrug and accept its losses but would defend Japanese property even if, in some cases, that meant resorting to the use of force. Japan has no resources of its own. What would happen if there were another oil shock or if the Arabs banded together and refused to sell oil to Japan?

No matter how much economic power a country has, it cannot achieve leadership without the military force to back it up. How else could Japan protect its factories that are scattered around the world or the foreign assets it has spent so much money to buy? What could Japan do to defend its interests against confiscations or freezes? Political coups and revolutions have not been eliminated from the world. Indeed, the dissolution of the Soviet Union and the end of the cold war have sparked a flurry of military uprisings in the new independent states. These civil wars can be explained by two basic forces, one *geoeconomic,* the other *geopolitical.* Geoeconomic forces rippling outward from a country trying to maximize its earning potential by going beyond its geographic borders are countered by a centripetal geopolitical force whereby groups within a country try to protect their own interests by identifying themselves as an independent nations. When the geopolitical force within a country is greater than the geoeconomic forces, civil wars such as the one in Bosnia are the net result.

Leadership means having the military capability to deal with all these risks. Right now the only country with that capability is the United States. The cost of leadership comes high. Is it really so necessary for Japan to become the dominant power? This should be where Japan can say "no." The Pax Japonica is only an illusion. Brzezinski's Amerippon is probably closer to future reality.

The Behavior of a Superpower. The suggestion that Japanese supremacy is an attainable dream surfaced intermittently in *The Japan That Can Say "No."* I have always believed that nothing can be achieved unless people are basically optimistic, but, where Japanese supremacy is concerned, I am a pessimist. This is one subject on which I can only say "no." Having lived and worked in the United States for more than thirty years, I am well aware of America's strength, the latent energy of the country that holds the leadership role. This is not something that can be shaken, as Shintaro Ishihara suggests, by bargaining with high tech or silicon chips.

American behavior might seem offensive to Japanese eyes, but it is simply the normal behavior of a country that has superpower status. There is a fundamental difference between a superpower and all the other countries in the world. On this matter, one particular memory has remained with me from my first visit to England in 1967. This was about the time when Japan was just overtaking Great Britain economically, yet the pride, arrogance, and offensiveness unique to a country that had long been the dominant power were still everywhere to be found.

A British colleague asked me whether I was an American or a Japanese. "What do you mean?" I asked. "Americans think only about money," he replied, "but we know that some things are more important than money." Britain was then showing the signs of a nation in decline, fretting about its rapid loss of ground to the United States. The proud vestiges of its former leadership status, however, still remained. Contemptuous of America's economic power, the British looked down on the United States as a country that knew only how to make money.

Japan finds itself in a similar position today. It too is regarded as a country that knows only how to make money, and its citizens are scorned as "economic animals." But having said that Japan is in the same position that America once occupied, I cannot go further and say that Japanese world leadership is also a possibility. The United States in those days had the world's strongest military power and a culture that it had inherited from Europe and had spread throughout the world. Japan today has neither military power nor a universally accepted value system. That is why it is sometimes called "a faceless country." Over the years I have advocated that Japan create an ideology, a Japanology, if you will, and not continue merely to make things and earn money. If it does not do so, but continues to behave as it has since World War II, far from becoming the supreme commander, it will end up just a rich noncommissioned officer.

When world leadership crossed the Atlantic, dominance in many other areas of activity also shifted from British to American hands. The study of economics was no exception; even academic disciplines cannot escape the influence of superpower politics. Britain is the birthplace of modern economics. Until world leadership shifted to the United States, there was a tendency among economists to believe that all the views held by British economists had to be correct. This assumption continued into the 1960s. When I went to Cambridge, the study of economics in England was in its final stages of brilliance, and British economists were extremely arrogant, haughtily confident that it was impossible to study economics anywhere outside Britain. Twenty-five years later, however, British economics has not retained even a trace of its former glory. During those years preeminence in the study of modern economics has shifted to the United States.

We Japanese are apt to forget that, although the United States may not be as all-powerful as it once was, it is still a superpower. Why are America's rules the best? Why do the Japanese have to follow them? The answer is always the same: because America is a superpower.

Paul Samuelson, the first American Nobel prizewinner in economics, regularly comes down from Boston to New York as a visiting professor at the Center for U.S.–Japan Business and Economic Studies. Samuelson and I are good friends and we argue a lot. One day I said, "If we were arguing in Japanese, I wouldn't lose," to which he laughingly responded, "Is English that difficult?" The truth of the matter is that in important discussions it is frustrating to use a language that is not your own. Japanese have a serious handicap in that regard. A superpower has the advantage in many ways. Its rules, language, and currency circulate freely throughout the world. No Japanese, however, can venture forth into the world without first acquiring some dollars and a command of English. Just as we change yen for dollars in the exchange market, we must continually translate from Japanese to English. This requires an enormous effort. The citizens of a superpower do not need to make any effort at all. They do not need translation machines in their heads, as other nationalities do. Americans enjoy the special privileges of world leadership.

In its dealings with the United States, Japan must not forget that America is a superpower and that superpowers have special privileges. It must also try to understand the feelings of a superpower that is in a state of relative decline. This does not mean being servile or submissively following America's lead. The relationship between the United States and Japan can be compared to the relationship between father and son or between older and younger brothers. A father has contradictory feelings—he frets at his declining strength and wants to assert his authority. A son should show respect and be understanding. When seen from Japan, a country that has never held world power, America's pride and arrogance certainly seem offensive. But it is even more difficult for America, which has reigned supreme for so long, to change its patterns of thought and action. The real reason that frictions between the United States and Japan have worsened lies in this fact.

If a just, impartial God really exists, and if he were asked to decide which side is playing fair—Japan or the United States—he might very well decide in favor of Japan. Since the war, Japan has undeviatingly followed the course laid out for it by America. It has worked hard to make good products and offer them cheaply to consumers worldwide, economized at home and saved its money, lived in peace and not gone to war. God might shake his head in wonder that Japan is now being criticized by the United States for following this course. But the logic of a superpower is like the logic of an aging father. A father will naturally criticize a son who disobeys him, but even when the son does exactly as he is told, the father will still criticize him if he poses a threat to the father's existence. A superpower can make any rules it likes; the Super 301 clause is a case in point. The United States naturally feels that the rest of the world "ought" to do as it says.

What can Japan do to eliminate that insulting "ought"? Barring Japan's fighting a war with America and winning, it is inconceivable that America would say to Japan—as Shintaro Ishihara seems to suggest—"You have beaten us technologically. Please help us out by selling us computer chips." A superpower does not operate in this way. Before it reached that point, it would put a freeze on Japan's assets or cut off its oil supply. It is naive to think that America would not go that far.

The lengths to which America will go can be seen in the policies it has used to contain the Soviet Union since World War II. Those excessive red witch hunts, the COCOM regulations, and the numerous economic sanctions have finally led to *perestroika.* The end of the cold war is a victory for United States world leadership. Now that communism has been defeated, what if the United States decides to focus all its attention on Japan? Should Japan once again "endure the unendurable" if the United States decides to punish Japan for what it believes to be unfair practices? Shintaro Ishihara can say "no" to that question, but I cannot. Instead I would ask what other options we have. We Japanese must exercise our imaginations. I will discuss my thoughts on this later, but one alternative would be for Japan to express itself clearly in negotiations with the United States and not behave manipulatively as when it uses foreign pressure *(gaiatsu)* as an excuse to enact unpopular, but prudent, domestic policies.

The Fading Reputation of Japanese Management

The Kanban *System: Tyranny over Subcontractors and Sub-subcontractors.* In the early 1980s Japanese management was highly touted in the United States, and American business schools scrambled to introduce courses on the subject. Now, however, Americans are interested only in certain features of Japanese management and no longer regard it as a model. Why this change in attitude? After careful analysis Americans came to realize that the efficiency of Japanese-style management is achieved at the expense of the Western concepts of life, liberty, and the pursuit of happiness.

Today when I ask students what Japanese management is, the more flattering replies are "lifetime employment," "the seniority system," and "labor-management collaboration." Some students, however, jokingly reply, "doing group exercises at three o'clock, then drinking with the boss, and singing *karaoke* after work." The myth of Japanese management has been shattered. To understand why, let's look at Toyota's *kanban* system, which was once made so much of in America.

The *kanban* system is, of course, a superbly efficient technique for minimizing inventory. If future demand were predictable, it would be possible to keep inventory to a minimum and supply only what is needed when it is needed—just in time. Since future demand cannot be perfectly predicted, however, there are two methods for dealing with it. The first is stockpiling finished goods—making what is necessary in advance and storing it in a warehouse until it is needed. The second is to assemble raw materials and whatever else is necessary and be fully prepared to respond instantly and make the required parts. If the latter method is completely implemented, inventory is reduced to zero because parts are considered to be inventory but raw materials are not. As a rule, three factor inputs must be kept in a state of readiness to make the system work: a labor force, capital, and raw materials. If all these can be kept on standby, goods can be made at any time.

Keeping labor on standby is difficult. Even a company like Toyota does not have the personnel to create a permanent standby unit. This is where the subcontractor and the sub-subcontractor come in. With a single telephone call from Toyota, the subcontractor and sub-subcontractor spring into action. The result is the "just-in-time" production system, that is, making only what will be sold at the time of the sale. In an extreme case, Toyota might put out an order for a 6:00 A.M. delivery at 6:00 P.M. or even 10:00 P.M. the night before, and the subcontractors and sub-subcontractors would have to work through the night to meet the deadline. Thus, Toyota is able to get the parts it wants, and only the parts it wants, when it wants them. This is possible because it has subcontractors and sub-subcontractors waiting on standby. These are the people who bear the brunt of the just-in-time system.

As an American commentator once noted, just-in-time is a system that could exist only in Japan. No matter how much the just-in-time method increases economic efficiency, introducing it into the United States would be impossible. What would happen if someone tried to place an order for a job at 6:00 P.M. on a Saturday or Sunday evening? The worker would say, "What time do you think it is?" and hang up. The just-in-time method is only possible if the social climate is suited to the *kanban* system, a social climate in which the weak can always be expected to work themselves to the bone at the request of the strong. This is an impossible demand to make in America. At first Americans thought the Toyota system was some sort of magic. But as Paul Samuelson once remarked to me, the Japanese are not gods; they do not know whether demand for cars will go up or down. Once Americans realized that the just-in-time method was not based on perfect predictions of future demand, but that it worked at the expense of the weak, the *kanban* system quickly lost its appeal.

When some of the glitter wore off Japanese management, questions also arose about Japan as a society that prized efficiency above all else and about whether personal happiness was being sacrificed to achieve it. In Western thinking, efficiency is not a moral value. Although it does not have negative connotations, Westerners do not believe that it takes precedence over everything else. Thus, Japanese-style efficiency is not a universal value and the means required to achieve it can even run counter to the values of Western society.

Ironically, the special characteristics that Japanese self-confidently believe are the motivating forces behind the miraculous growth of the Japanese economy are singled out by Westerners as unfair, inhuman, and not universally valid. Japanese, for example, take justifiable pride in the Shinkansen Bullet train because it is safe, comfortable, and always on time. It is the visible embodiment of Japanese perfectionism, their tendency to put 120 percent effort into everything they do. But, then, Japan's entire transportation system, right down to the old trains in the remote countryside, generally runs on time. There are few countries in the world where you can literally set your clock by the regularly scheduled trains. The quality of Japan's train service is certainly something to be proud of, but the downside of this Japanese obsession with punctuality may well lead to such inhuman behavior as that of the teacher at a Hyogo Prefecture high school who in the summer of 1990 automatically shut the school gates at the sound of the bell and killed a student as she tried to enter. If punctuality is given precedence over everything else, discretion and good judgment are lost. This is a peculiarity of the Japanese that Americans cannot understand.

Schools are not the only Japanese institutions that do not tolerate lateness. American young people who have worked as trainees for Japanese corporations cannot understand why Japanese office workers are almost excessively punctual, arriving at work on time only to sit around drinking tea and reading the paper once they are there. This is one example of how rules and authority are given precedence over all other considerations, but there are many others. Americans are at first impressed but subsequently repelled by Japanese pedestrians' absolute obedience to traffic signals. A lone pedestrian will stand waiting at an intersection for the light to change even when there are no cars in sight. "Why not install traffic lights that can be controlled by push-buttons depending on the time of day?" they will say. "Crossing the street when you know it is safe to do so is common sense by U.S. thinking, even if the light is red. For a woman alone late at night it can even be dangerous to wait for the light to change."

One of the reasons Americans say Japanese democracy is odd is that it tends to be too efficient. Adopting a single industrial policy, for example, is efficient. First, high-level bureaucrats devise a plan, to which no one makes any objections. Why not? Because the plan is absolutely correct. Why is it correct? Because every aspect of it has the clear objective of achieving the number one position. Devising the best and most efficient means to implement the plan comes next. Once the details have been worked out, orders immediately trickle down from above. This American view of Japan underlies the revisionists' argument that Japan is different. This efficient system has nothing democratic about it, they complain; it is totalitarian.

Looked at from this perspective, Japanese democracy certainly does seem odd. It certainly does seem to operate at the expense of "life, liberty, and the pursuit of happiness." Western-style democracies are, in fact, more inefficient social systems than democracy in Japan. They operate on the principle that a society that functions under the command of a king or a feudal lord may be efficient, but when it comes to the greatest good of the greatest number, one would have to choose democracy no matter how inefficient it is. For the sake of this principle the heads of kings have rolled and the blood of many citizens has been spilled.

The tragedy at the Hyogo Prefecture high school was given a great deal of coverage by the Japanese mass media during the summer of 1990. One commentator made the statement that the incident was proof that there was no relationship of trust between student and school. That someone in a position to have his opinions broadcast throughout Japan could be so obtuse infuriates me. Few seem to realize that the school gate incident, observance of traffic lights, punctual trains, and workaholics living in rabbit hutches are all bound together by a single thread. The power of organizations such as schools or corporations is so great in Japan that they take precedence over everything else. Setting aside the question of whether or not a me-centered society like the West's is ideal, a value system that puts the priorities of organizations ahead of human needs will continue to come in for strong criticism from the rest of the world in the years ahead.

Japan Is the Land of the Leveraged Buyout (LBO). A prime example of the management practices that America is now reevaluating is the Japanese system of cross-shareholding, which was raised as an issue in the Structural Impediments Initiative talks. America is obsessed with this issue because although Japanese can freely buy almost any U.S. company they want, the cross-shareholding system prevents Americans from buying Japanese companies.

The leveraged buyout is a widespread practice in the United States. Simply put, an LBO turns a public company into a private company. Suppose, for example, that I buy up all of General Motor's stocks and make it into my own privately owned corporation. To do that I would need an enormous amount of money, which I would borrow from a bank using as collateral General Motor's factories which I one day expect to own. The difference between a leveraged buyout and a merger and acquisition is that an LBO makes all the stock in a company someone's private property, thereby removing the stock from public sale and converting a company listed on the stock exchange into an unlisted company. In a merger and acquisition the company being bought becomes part of the purchaser's company, or a subsidiary, or a separate company, but it does not become private.

LBOs have been popular in the United States because in some instances the benefits of being a private company outweigh those of being a public one. The public stock system was developed to allow industrialists to accumulate capital at low risk. The original idea behind the stock market system was to diversify the risk by offering stocks widely for public sale. In other words, if a loss is incurred, each stockholder theoretically suffers only a small loss. On that score, an LBO is extremely risky except when it involves a company with a healthy cash flow. A company with an easy liquidity position is strong.

In 1988, after the management of R.J.R. Nabisco announced its intention to attempt a leveraged buyout, Kohlberg, Kravis, Roberts and Company, a large holding company, launched one instead. R.J.R. Nabisco had been formed by the merger of a tobacco company, R.J. Reynolds Industries, and a cookie-making company, Nabisco Brands. The merger of these two totally unrelated companies was motivated by the fact that tobacco is regarded as a social evil in America and has a bad image. If a tobacco company also made a family-oriented product that everyone likes such as cookies, it would improve its corporate image. The merger resulted in enormous growth for R.J.R. Nabisco, the reasons for which are not hard to understand. Tobacco may be considered a social evil, but once people start smoking they find it hard to quit. Thus tobacco sells well. Cookies are a recession-proof product that sells no matter how badly the economy does. The combination of these two companies produced a bulging cash flow, which was an enormous attraction for others. The inevitable happened—Kravis launched a leveraged buyout.

The advantages of a leveraged buyout are that, as both proprietor and sole shareholder, one does not have to worry about getting fired or about outsiders attempting a takeover through a merger and acquisition. The proprietor does not have to pay out a lot of dividends because he, not the shareholders, owns the company. This allows him to think about keeping his employees happy and makes possible stable, long-term management. If there is any cause for concern, it is the fact that the risks are not diversified, but as long as the cash flow continues, there is no need to worry.

In the United States, where M&As happen all the time, corporate executives are always anxious about the possibility of a takeover. Every morning American CEOs are riveted to their computer screens, analyzing the latest data on their companies' performance. If stock prices go down, they worry about an M&A, and they always keep an eye out for any large purchases of their companies' stock. Although CEOs earn high salaries, the pressure on them is enormous. The leveraged buyout was developed to counter M&As. The logic behind the LBO is simple: A public company can become the target of an M&A; if a company is private, there is absolutely no such worry.

Japan's cross-shareholding system is an indirect form of leveraged buyout. In Japan only 20 or 30 percent of a company's stock is actually traded; the remaining 70 or 80 percent is held by the owner of the company or by affiliated banks, insurance companies, and big businesses referred to as "stable stockholders." American commentators often use the Japanese word *keiretsu* to describe this system of joint stockholding between companies and their main banks and other companies they do business with. The creation of these corporate groupings means that member companies do not have to go outside the group to procure parts or financing or technological assistance. As in other Japanese groups, the keiretsu has a vertical hierarchy and the parent company has a privileged position vis-à-vis its subsidiaries and subcontractors. This sort of group relationship among companies has many advantages, as some American firms have begun to realize. As long as it does not interfere with a company's freedom of action, it enables group members to wield considerable power in terms of efficiency, stability, and cost reduction.

Cross-shareholding within a corporate group is a way for member companies to hold stock in one another's firms to prevent them from going on the market. It was created because at one time takeovers and attempts to buy controlling interests in companies were also commonplace in Japan. Something had to be done to limit the circulation of a company's stock. Under Japanese law it is illegal to hold stock in one's own company, so cross-shareholding was devised as a last resort. In effect, one company president says to another, "If you hold 20 percent of the shares in my company, I'll hold 20 percent of the shares in yours." If several companies hold each other's stocks in this way, a group of stable stockholders is soon created, all of whom abide by the unwritten law that no one will sell another company's stock for speculation. The fact that the stock cannot be sold has the same effect as the company's holding the stock itself. Because shares are held in the names of the stable stockholders, the law is not violated, but management is in effect holding 70 or 80 percent of its own company's stock. Cross-shareholding has practically all the advantages of an

LBO: An American-style merger and acquisition is out of the question.

Cross-shareholding Is the Reason for Japan's High Stock Prices. The excessively high price of stocks in Japan in the late 1980s was a direct result of the cross-shareholding system. If only 20 or 30 percent of a company's stock ever comes onto the market, this inadequate supply naturally pushes up the price. Because of these high prices, the common international yardstick, the price/earnings ratio, was excessively high in Japan, and nowhere else. This again feeds the Japan-is-different argument.

Additionally, because management is in effect holding 70 or 80 percent of the stock in its own company, there is no need, as there is in the United States, to worry about stockholders. Thus, dividends can be kept low. By holding stock dividends to moderate levels, management can keep its employees happy and adopt long-term strategies—"look ten years ahead," as Akio Morita puts it. This is impossible in America. A listed company in America puts nearly 80 percent of its stock on the market for public sale, and this stock constantly changes hands. That means that U.S. executives cannot ignore the wishes of their stockholders. They must raise performance levels and increase dividends because American stockholders will not wait patiently for results. If corporate performance deteriorates, the CEO is soon fired.

Japanese executives are critical of American business people for looking only "ten minutes ahead." It is not a matter of not looking ahead, however, but of not being able to look ahead. This is the true nature of the stock market system. Japanese companies are proud of their long-term, stable management, but from a Western perspective, this is possible only because Japanese companies are, in effect, private companies.

In *The Japan That Can Say "No"* Chairman Morita wrote the following:

When our factory in California started in 1972, it employed about two hundred and fifty local people. Then the oil shock happened in 1973, and business conditions deteriorated for companies throughout the world. The California plant was hard hit. There was not enough work to keep two hundred and fifty employees busy full time. The president of Sony America, an American, came to me and said that there was no way out except layoffs. But I said "no." We hired these people, and we are going to keep them; we'll send money from the parent company to keep all two hundred and fifty of them. If we can't maintain a daily production schedule, we will use the remaining time for training. The employees were very enthusiastic about this idea. They came to feel that the plant was their home, and they did what American employees never do—they kept their work stations cleaned and polished. This became the nucleus of our California plant. Today, it has about 1,500 employees, and they have never tried to form a union.

Sony was able to avoid layoffs because, in essence, it is a private company. American executives would like to treat their employees well and would not resort to layoffs if they could avoid them. If corporate performance deteriorates, however, and the stockholders get angry and withdraw their money, what else can they do? The very survival of the company is at stake. They may lose everything. That is why they treat stockholders with more consideration than employees.

The United States put Japan's cross-shareholding system on the agenda of the Structural Impediments Initiative talks not simply because American companies cannot buy Japanese companies, but because Americans believe that, by allowing the trading of stocks between companies or groups of companies, Japan is supporting a boycott against America. Cross holding stock for the sake of long-term, stable management is not an internationally accepted practice. America contends that it is unfair because it applies only to business deals within Japan and deviates from the fundamental principles of capitalism.

Japan: The Bubble Superpower

What's Fair in Japan Is Unfair in the Rest of the World. U.S.–Japanese economic disputes surfaced in earnest in the early 1980s. Although criticized for its piecemeal response to American demands, which has been likened to the peeling of an onion, Japan has been slowly instituting reforms. Japan's market today should be approaching the standards desired by the United States and Europe, and foreign criticisms should be abating. In fact, however, foreign criticisms seem to be growing more intense: Japan's rules are unfair; Japan is a closed society. Japan-bashing in America has been gearing up instead of slowing down. Why is Japan the object of so much criticism?

The differences between the United States with its two-hundred-year history and Japan with its two-thousand-year history underlie the economic friction between the two countries. One of the major themes of

American history is the filling up of open spaces. American history is one of nation-building and entrepreneurship—the pioneering of the vast American continent from coast to coast and the invention of new technologies and new types of business. One might say it is a story of economic prosperity attained through the conquest of nature.

This achievement required an enormous population. That is why the population of the United States rose, in seventy-five years' time, from 100 million in 1917 to nearly 250 million today; that is also why the country has become a "salad bowl." To fill up all its open spaces, America opened itself up to immigrants of all races and nationalities. As we've already seen, governing such a country requires a clear and fair set of rules. America's concern with fair rules is the result of the principles on which it was founded.

Japan's history, on the other hand, is that of a closed society on a small island that for the past two thousand years has tried to keep outsiders out. Japan might be called a nepotistic society where regional or family ties enter into all considerations, and where people from the same town or graduates of the same school are given preferential treatment. In Japanese government agencies and major corporations, for example, an "old boy" network of graduates from each of the leading universities is at work to ensure that alumni from their school get promoted. If we look at today's U.S.–Japan trade disputes from this perspective, we might say they are the result of a collision between a traditionally closed society and a traditionally open one. Japan needs to understand that America's talk about unfair rules is rooted in the American frontier spirit and dates back to a time when, in order to fill up the open spaces—both literal and figurative—of a new society on a new continent, the rules had to be simple, clear, and broadly based, with the details to be filled in later. Until Japan understands this fact, U.S.–Japan relations will continue to go nowhere.

For the most part, Japanese are surprisingly ignorant or, even worse, indifferent about America. Most seemingly informed discussions of America are simply a repetition of preconceived ideas without regard to detail. The criticism that U.S. management looks only ten minutes ahead is an example of this lack of understanding. Relationships in an open society are, by their very nature, short-term and fluctuating. If an American worker discovers that another firm offers better benefits, he or she will think nothing of quitting and accepting the better job. This is normal and natural in an open society. The ability of people to move around freely helps to create a rational, unsentimental society unfettered by any ties. That is how the vast, open spaces are filled in. That is why Shane, in the movie of that name, will never come back but must move on to some new open space. If Shane stayed on and became the town sheriff, he would lose his mythic significance.

Japan is just the opposite. The strong group ties of the Japanese have often been traced back to the days when Japan was a country of rice farmers. Wet-field rice cultivation is highly dependent on the cooperative efforts of the entire community. Japan is a society where relationships of trust can be established only on the assumption that they will continue for a long time to come. Computer companies make ridiculously low bids for new contracts in the knowledge that once a contract has been won it will be profitable for the long term. Lifetime employment is another example of this way of thinking. Long-term, unchanging relationships are the props that support Japanese society.

The reason for this emphasis on taking a long-term view is that Japan does not have the open spaces America does. Japan is a country with a high arrest rate. This fact, too, is related to its being a closed society. In a society that operates on the principle of keeping outsiders out, criminals have no place to run to and are soon caught. America, on the other hand, offers open spaces even to its criminals. If a criminal in Massachusetts flees to neighboring Rhode Island, for example, the Massachusetts police cannot cross the state line to apprehend him. That is why American law enforcement agencies have a double structure involving state and local police, on the one hand, and the Federal Bureau of Investigation, on the other. In order to maintain an open society, one must be willing to pay the commensurate costs.

From the American perspective, Japan's long-term relationships appear to be designed to exclude outsiders. Americans regard it as normal for a company to conclude a contract with a French company one day, but if a Japanese firm comes along the next day with a better product, to switch over to the company that offers the better goods. This very trait, in fact, has allowed Japan to conquer the U.S. market. Japanese relations, built on long-term trust, are not so flexible. No matter how good an American product may be, an American company will probably not gets its foot in the door because the Japanese distributor has a long-standing relation with Matsushita or some other Japanese firm. To add insult to injury, the American company may be given the useless advice that "if you want to do business in Japan, you must first build up personal relationships. Trust is something that develops slowly over time."

The Japanese attitude toward relationships is the direct opposite of the American attitude. While it is true that the United States is able to think only ten minutes ahead and Japan thinks ten years ahead, this very fact could be used as proof of the impermeability and exclusivity of Japan, which will use the ten years to establish a monopolistic relationship and make it impossible for newcomers to get in, no matter how hard they try. What could be better proof of this than the revelation in the fall of 1989 that two Japanese computer firms were being investigated for making "one-yen bids" (in one case, the figure was later revised to 1.45 million yen) to secure highly profitable contracts for prefectural computer systems. The lesson this incident teaches is that a long-term, monopolistic contract is far more advantageous than immediate profits. Taking a short-term loss to secure a long-term profit is regarded as natural in Japan, but Americans regard it as a prime example of unfair Japanese business practices.

I was once consulted by an executive of an American insurance company that wanted to branch out into Japan. "We have developed a new insurance product," he told me, "but when we approached the Japanese Ministry of Finance about selling it in Japan, we were refused permission on the grounds that the insurance was totally new, and thus it was unfair to the other insurance companies in Japan that had no knowledge of the product. If we wanted to sell in Japan, we would have to reveal the entire nature of the insurance to Japanese insurance companies. Once all companies were able to start at the same point it would be fair, and it would be possible for us to get permission. How can a country like this call itself a free economy that believes in the principles of competition?"

The insurance company executive's surprise and consternation were obvious. In the United States, the government will approve any new product as long as it poses no danger and its purposes are not antisocial. The first company that can get that product onto the market will naturally prevail. The insurance company, which had made a substantial effort to come up with a new idea, was naturally disconcerted to be told that its product would have to be made available to rival companies. This episode clearly demonstrates the difference in business practices between the two countries. Americans find it inconceivable that producers are more highly regarded than consumers in Japan and that companies are asked to reveal the know-how they have gone to great lengths to develop. These attitudes are regarded as antithetical to the competitive principles of a capitalist economy.

To my regret, I had to say to the insurance executive: "I am sorry, but there is nothing I can do. The Japanese authorities ignore consumers and protect producers. They line up all the corporations in a particular sector at the starting line and say, 'Ready, go.' The authorities' responsibility is getting everyone to the starting line. If companies drop out afterwards, it is not their responsibility. But if they don't get everyone off to the same start and a serious problem arises in the future, the official in charge will be held responsible." It is not without cause that America pushed the interests of the consumer to the forefront of the Structural Impediments Initiative talks.

The Mystery of Japanese Stock Inflation. The phrase "stock economy" became popular in Japan in the late 1980s to describe a type of economy in which the growth of asset prices is greater than the growth of the GNP. Although it was certainly possible to describe the Japanese economy in that way, what actually happened was the formation of an asset bubble, that is, "stock inflation." During the 1980s stock inflation occurred in the United States, too, but the pace was incomparably slower than in Japan. Although Japanese assets increased in value, the development of an excessive asset bubble that threatened to destroy the balance with the GNP was by no means desirable.

In general, when the word *inflation* is used in newspapers and elsewhere, it refers to "flow inflation," that is, the inflation in the cost of consumer goods and capital goods that most closely affect our everyday lives. The word *stock* refers to land, stocks, bonds, and other assets that will not disappear within a year. If, as the word implies, *flow* refers to things like water that disappear, *stock* can be likened to a river bed. When inflation occurs in stock, it also occurs in flow, which derives from stock. For example, if the price of land rises, the price of condominiums and the rent on apartments built on the land go up as well. In the case of Japan's stock inflation, however, this did not happen. Although the land in and around Tokyo nearly doubled in value between 1985 and 1989, housing prices did not double.

This was not necessarily a bad thing, but we need to consider the reasons for it.

But first, why did land prices skyrocket in a matter of a very few years? Half of the reason lies with Japan and half with the United States. To be specific, America imports too much from Japan and Japan exports too much. As a result, Japan acquired an enormous reserve and this led to excess liquidity. When a huge trade surplus continued for several years in the 1980s, more dollars entered Japan than could possibly be spent. Of course, Japan could put the money into dollar savings accounts or buy U.S. treasury bills, but it was impossible to use up all the dollars it had earned. Japan, therefore, converted them to yen and was still glutted with money.

America went on printing dollars and buying Japanese goods and Japan kept on selling goods. As a result, dollars flooded uncontrollably into Japan. If the Japanese economy worked the way the textbooks say it should, Japan ought to have experienced severe inflation as a result of this excessive liquidity, but that did not happen because Japan is a country where the propensity to save is exceptionally strong and consumer spending, especially spending on imports, is exceptionally weak. If the money glut did not go into consumption, where did it go? The answer is: into buying land and stocks in Japan and land and companies abroad. This is why between 1985 and 1990 Japanese land and stock prices soared. This situation is what I call "stock inflation" or "asset price inflation," but for some reason people in Japan avoided using the word "inflation" and talked instead about "entering the age of a stock economy" or of Japan as a "stock superpower." This was glossing over an unhealthy and unbalanced condition. As long as the Japanese government chose to emphasize a way of looking at the situation that conveyed only half the truth, it was not able to make the Japanese people aware of the seriousness of the problem or prepare them for the rapid disinflation Japan experienced when the bubble finally burst.

When applied to daily consumption, the word "inflation" has a very bad image. But when inflation occurs in land and stocks, since these are not essentials of daily life, the people who do not own them are indifferent and those who do become very rich. Although what happened in Japan in the late 1980s was stock inflation, it was inflation nonetheless. The disparity between the haves and the have-nots that it created provoked a hard-to-dispel sense of poverty and dissatisfaction among middle managers who were in the prime of their working careers. Ninety-nine percent of the individuals who own land, however, do not use it for business purposes or for speculation. They neither buy nor sell.

Most Japanese cannot sell their land, no matter how high the price goes. If they sold, they would have nowhere to live. Selling one's land would be as unwise as selling one's loincloth *(fundoshi)*. Although it is theoretically possible to have several loincloths, the ordinary person has only one so he sets great value on it. When the value of land goes up, exactly the same reasoning applies, but few ever think in these terms. On the contrary, people are delighted because they think, "My land has gone up in value. I could not buy it now. I bought at a good time." But if they do not sell, no matter how much the value has increased, nothing else has really changed. Even if they do sell and get a high price for their land, it will cost them even more to buy an equivalent piece of property. There are taxes when they sell and taxes when they buy, and their real estate tax will go up, so there are no advantages in selling. But as long as the asset bubble lasts, landowners feel that they have become rich. That is the illusion of stock inflation. That is also why stock inflation does not spread to consumer goods, that is, to flow.

The vast majority of Japan's Liberal Democratic party supporters have splendid loincloths, so if the politicians had tinkered with the existing real estate laws, they would have lost votes. Although they had adopted policies that caused land prices to double in a mere two or three years, politicians were unable to devise any appropriate measures to cope with the situation. The Liberal Democratic party kept saying that something should be done about land prices, but, in fact, it did nothing because so many of its members thought they had good loincloths. Moreover, if the price of land were to go down, the big banks that provided the financing would be seriously affected, as in fact they have been.

The "New Rich" Phenomenon. This sort of situation cannot last for very long, however. As often happens in economics, if an imbalance occurs, there is inevitably a movement to correct it. Just as it is impossible to eat too much rich food without suffering a weight gain or even developing cirrhosis of the liver, it is impossible for stock and only stock to become excessively inflated. In the normal course of things, something happens to stop the rise in the price of land and stock market shares.

As a general rule, when the price of land stops rising, the prices of other commodities catch up to restore a balance. Over the years Japan has experienced several periods of runaway inflation in land prices. During the administration of Prime Minister Kakuei Tanaka (1972–1974), the government spent too much money on a plan to "remodel the Japanese archipelago," a massive public works program aimed at developing the Japanese countryside for industrial expansion. This caused the price of land to shoot up. But eventually the land stopped selling, and the price rise came to a halt. Then, slowly, incomes began to rise until ten or fifteen years later people were able to buy land again. This is the normal pattern that this process follows.

But Japan's trade surplus has been both huge and long-standing. As a result, the money glut had no place to go and the unprecedented happened: The rise in Tokyo's land prices spread to the rest of the country. It was as if Japan were suffering from a cancer that metastasized: The body loses its strength and can do nothing but wait to die. Foremost among the signs that this was happening in Japan was what is known as the "new rich" phenomenon, which is fundamentally changing the egalitarian society that Japan has created since the end of the war. Of course, it was a good thing for the people who became more affluent, but it has also enormously magnified the gap in incomes and living standards between those who got rich and those who did not. This definitely cannot be considered a plus for the future vitality of Japan.

Someone once told me an interesting story. In front

of Keio University, one of the top private universities in downtown Tokyo, there used to be an old and rather mediocre sushi shop where many Keio students went to eat cheap sushi. When the price of land went up recently, the sushi shop owner sold the property for several billion yen. He bought a house, a place in the country, and an imported car. In a complete turnabout the owner of a mediocre sushi shop had become a member of the nouveaux riches.

This man's good fortune is a matter for congratulations. The problem lies in the structure of the economy that it reflects. The people who once ate cheap sushi in that shop studied hard and became leaders of Japan's political and financial world. But no matter how hard they work, no matter how great their services to Japan, they will earn only about one or two hundred million yen in their lifetimes. Half of that will be taken up by taxes, and when they retire, it is doubtful that they will have a hundred million yen left. To cite a pun making the rounds, in Tokyo you can't buy a *mansion* for that kind of money, let alone an *oku-sion.**

When the new rich phenomenon occurs, talented people who have a real contribution to make to Japan lose the will to work. Until recently all Japanese claimed to belong to the middle class. When they looked at their neighbors and saw there was not too much difference between them, they were willing to work just a little bit harder in the belief that they could get ahead. It became a point of pride when Japan was

Mansion is the Japanese term for a condominium. *Oku-sion* is an invented word. The pun plays on the word *man* (in *mansion*), which means ten thousand in Japanese, and *oku*, which means hundred million.

called an economic superpower, and when Japanese heard that an American white-collar worker owned a house with a swimming pool, it did not mean much and no one felt jealous. Popular comparisons that likened Americans to the proverbial spendthrift grasshopper only served to make them work even harder. But then they saw the people next door sell the tiny strip of land their parents owned in the Tokyo area for several billion yen and become members of the new rich. This is bound to do considerable damage to Japanese morale, to the political base, and to the will to work and is likely to become a serious issue in the future.

For Tokyo residents who own no land, owning a home of their own has become an unattainable dream unless they move far out of the city. They have probably not been sorry to see the price of land plummet in the past two years, but the people who are suffering most during the present disinflationary period are those with low incomes. In the long run, it will be a nearly impossible task to restore the situation to what it once was and eliminate the gap between rich and poor. The very strengths that have made Japan an economic superpower—its Japanese-style fairness and egalitarianism, its skilled and diligent work force— may be lost. The high land prices that made Japan into a global asset-holding superpower also hold this explosive potential at home.

The End of the Bubble Economy

Collapse from Within. On the last trading day of the 1980s, December 29, 1989, the Japanese stock market stood at 38,915 points. Slightly more than a year and a half later on July 18, 1992, the Nikkei index had plummeted to 14,309 and Japan was headed into recession. It is a truism to say that the present recession in Japan was caused by the end of the bubble economy. The point I would like to make, however, is that a distinction needs to be made between this recession and the ones that have preceded it. Previous recessions have been triggered by some kind of external shock; the present recession was caused by factors within the Japanese economy itself.

The recession of 1971, for example, was caused by the "Nixon shock"—the announcement by President Nixon in 1971 that the dollar would no longer be convertible to gold. At the time the International Monetary Fund was established, the dollar was pegged to gold at a price of thirty-five dollars to the ounce. When America's balance of payments began to show a deficit and gold flowed out of the country in huge quantities, however, the United States decided to go off the gold standard, thus forcing the revaluation of currencies throughout the world. Japan was particularly affected; with the yen-dollar exchange rate no longer fixed at 360 yen to the dollar, the yen strengthened dramatically with adverse effects on the Japanese economy.

The first oil shock two or three years later dealt the Japanese economy another severe blow, but as we shall see in chapter 6, Japan was not only able to deal successfully with the recession and inflation that resulted from a rise in oil prices, it actually came out the stronger for it. That was certainly the case at the time of the second oil shock in 1979–80 when Japan made use of its earlier experiences to emerge in the 1980s as a major economic power. The Plaza Accord in 1985 was another externally caused setback, but as I have already discussed in chapter 1, Japan was soon able to overcome the problems caused by the strong yen. In fact, U.S. pressure on Japan to expand domestic demand stimulated the Japanese economy and made it even stronger.

As a result, a bubble economy was created and eventually that bubble burst. Business has deteriorated even for blue chip Japanese companies such as automakers; Nissan, for example, has been forced to close one of its main high-tech factories. Major computermakers and producers of consumer electronics are all suffering, and steel companies have been slashing their work forces. Japan has fallen into a recession of major proportions unlike anything it has experienced in the postwar period. This time, however, the recession was not caused by an external shock but rather by causes within the Japanese economy and thus it is quite different in nature from the recessions that preceded it.

The collapse of the bubble economy has also been accompanied by a series of distinctly Japanese scandals in both the financial and the political worlds. One of the first of these to surface was the revelation that some of Japan's major security companies were compensating favored clients for their investment losses. Here was another blatant example of Japan's hypercorporatism—the corporate structure that protects large, long-term clients at the expense of the consumer, or in this case, the small investor. More revelations followed—the Sagawa Kyubin kickback scandal, links between government officials, big business, and organized crime, and the arrest of Liberal Democratic party "fixer" Shin Kanemaru. Cash payments to Japanese politicians are nothing new or, for that matter, newsworthy, but even the most hardened cynics have been astonished at the sums involved in the Kanemaru case. The recent series of scandals has been criticized worldwide and Japanese politics has become an object of derision.

Right now Japanese-style capitalism presents a sorry sight to the world for many reasons. But the United States, Britain, and other countries with advanced capitalist systems have all gone through similar experiences in the early stages of their development. No country has had a textbook-perfect system of capitalism right from the very beginning. In this sense, Japan is not unique. Criticisms of Japan's late-blooming capitalism by mature capitalist countries have been quite severe, but that does not mean that they themselves have never had similar scandals or similar economic bubbles. The U.S. economy has already gone through the experiences that Japan is now facing; it can be compared to a somewhat older graduate of the same school of hard knocks, now older and wiser, who is apt to deny that he might not have always done all the right things himself when he was young.

Japanese-Style Capitalism. To understand how the bubble economy developed in Japan we first need to understand how banks and countries generate money. Some people have suggested that a monetary system in which all business deals are conducted in cash would prevent the risks of a bubble economy. There is a grain of truth in that suggestion. If the money supply was determined by the amount of hard currency a country had and every time it bought something it would have to draw on its cash reserves, the possibility of a bubble economy developing would be reduced. The problem is that the limited supply of money would make it difficult to build new factories, put in new equipment, or make the other real investments needed to make goods to sell. In short, a monetary system based on hard currency prevents an economy from making adequate use of its productive capacity. That is, in fact, why a gold or silver standard has become obsolete and has been replaced by credit.

Although in the long run, the way capitalism works in the United States and Japan is not very different, there are differences in certain aspects of both systems. One of these areas is the way the two economies expand credit. Japanese-style capitalism is a form of capitalism that might be called an assets or a "land standard" system. In this system, assets come first and banks play the leading role. Banks use assets—primarily land—as collateral to create the credit from which earnings are generated. These earnings are channeled back into greater asset formation, on which the banks once again make huge loans, and this process is the engine that powers the Japanese economy. This type of economic behavior led to rampant asset inflation during the bubble economy period. Land used as security to borrow money created huge quantities of credit, which in turn sent the money supply soaring. Loans in Europe and North America are also backed by mortgages taken out on homes and factories, but no other country in the world uses land as collateral to the extent that Japan does. The enormous money supply created by these land-backed loans sometimes goes into "flow"—consumer goods and investments—and the result is inflation in the ordinary sense of the word, but in this case it went into the purchase of more assets and the result was an asset bubble and what I have earlier called "stock inflation."

Lack of resources is of course the conditioning factor behind Japanese-style capitalism. Because Japan has no natural resources of its own, businesses there are of the type that provide goods and services to the consumer. Japanese companies, therefore, must use their assets to create capital, which is then put to work to acquire earnings. In Japan a network of big banks backed by the government (the Bank of Japan and the Ministry of Finance) is spread throughout the country. Because Japanese businesses are run with money borrowed from banks using real estate as collateral, the main bank's say in the business world is enormous. Furthermore, the fact that the government is behind the big banks' free creation of credit has given rise to the myth that there can never be a bank failure. Big Japanese-style banks which operate in this manner do not exist in Europe or North America. With a few exceptions, American banks, by comparison, are merely local banks that carry on small-scale financing. In resource-rich America the capital that is highly valued is not assets but working capital and there is little need for real-estate-secured bank borrowing. The political and economic climate does not allow for the creation of big banks on a Japanese scale, and banks do not have the same kind of status that they do in Japan.

Land and the Bubble Economy. The end of the bubble economy finally laid to rest the myth that the price of stocks and other assets may go down but the price of land in Japan will always go up. The reason the present recession is fundamentally different from earlier recessions caused by external shocks is that this time the value of land in some areas has fallen by 20 to 30 percent. As we have seen, Prime Minister Tanaka's plans to remodel the Japanese archipelago also caused land prices to soar in the early 1970s. When that bubble burst, land stopped selling but its value did not go down to the extent that it has today. The rise in land prices came to a halt, real estate stopped selling, and over time both income and earnings slowly went up so that ten years later the balance was restored. Then, asset prices began to rise once again, land began to be sold, and the economy prospered.

When an economy is running smoothly, the ratio of income to assets remains constant. This is what Professor Paul Samuelson and I call the "law of economic conservation." In the case of the American economy, the ratio of GNP or GDP to total assets or total wealth between 1950 and 1990 has been 0.33. To put it another way, in the United States three units of assets are required to generate one unit of income. This ratio of 3 to 1 has continued almost unchanged since World War II, through the so-called golden age of the 1960s, the post-Vietnam period of high inflation, the soaring asset prices of the 1970s, and the oil shocks at the beginning of the 1980s. Deviations from this 0.33 average have been very slight.

Although a comparison of the earnings to assets ratios for all the OECD countries has not yet been completed, the figures for Canada are nearly the same as those for the United States. They fluctuate between

0.33 and 0.29 with an average of 0.31. Even for Britain, the rate between 1950 and 1990 is in the range of 0.25.

If we look at trends in the ratio of GNP to total wealth in Japan, however, the situation changes dramatically. The figures go from 0.255 in 1955 to 0.247 in 1970 and finally to 0.179 in 1991; in other words, the average rate of return on assets has declined to almost 12 percent. Compared with America, where a stable rate of return on assets of around 30 percent has always been maintained, this figure is astonishingly low and shows the extremely unstable and fragile side of the Japanese economy, which is normally believed to be so robust. Indeed, in this area there is a fundamental difference between Japanese capitalism and the capitalism practiced in the industrialized countries of Europe and North America.

As long as assets in Japan play the role they do, Japanese capitalism will probably continue to be asset-oriented, but when the return on assets becomes as excessively low as it did at the height of the bubble economy, reason will dictate an economic correction. The crash of the stock market should be seen as an adjustment to Japan's unbalanced earnings to assets ratio.

In the past the mechanisms to bring earnings in line with assets were quite different from what has happened in the past two or three years. Until now the pattern had been that first real estate values went up, then after a while they stopped rising and waited for earnings to catch up. This time, however, because the rise in asset prices was too steep for earnings to be able to catch up, prices began to come down of their own accord.

In any event the bubble economy has come to an end, and the Japanese economy, like the European and American economies, now has to deal with an internally generated boom-and-bust cycle. Banks are tottering, brokerages are going bankrupt, even Japan's strongest manufacturing companies are going through hard times. Perhaps the economy will improve only to slip back into recession again, but ultimately the economy will prosper. Capitalism has its periods of prosperity and recession. During the boom periods some people become enormously rich; when the boom comes to an end some go bankrupt. Just as people go through many ups and downs in the course of their lives so do businesses, but in the long run the economy as a whole improves. That is what the capitalist system is all about. Some may wonder whether it would be more efficient to plan everything and make the economy run according to plan instead of having a market-oriented system. Economies based on plans made by fallible human beings may at first seem to run smoothly but the collapse of socialism in Eastern Europe and the Soviet Union has shown that they are in fact even more fragile than economies that are left to the workings of market forces.

The failures of an economy simply prove that human beings are not perfect. Everyone makes mistakes. Companies, like people, try various things and sometimes they fail, but they make use of what they learn from their experiences and try again.

SIX

JAPAN'S FUTURE COURSE

Is Japan Really a Technological Superpower?

Product Innovation versus Process Innovation. Has Japan really become such a technological superpower that it can, as Shintaro Ishihara claims, twist America and Russia around its little finger by controlling the flow of its high-tech exports? Or is Japan's technological status still comparatively minor? Is the U.S. criticism that Japan is weak in the area of basic research still justified, and is the argument that, when it comes to technology, Japan has had a "free ride" correct? Both these views are probably right, but both are also probably wrong.

Technological development should be thought of as a flow or a cycle that has two phases. The first is the discovery of new technology in the true sense of the term, that is, technology that leads to new products. This is what is known as "product innovation." The second is technological progress made by improving

183

upon or refining product innovations. This is called "process innovation." Roughly speaking, the world economy has seen two waves of technological development since World War II—the twenty-year period of product innovation during the 1950s and 1960s that was centered in the United States, and the twenty-year period of process innovation in the 1970s and 1980s that built on this earlier period and was centered mainly in Japan.

What can we expect to happen in the 1990s and the early twenty-first century? Of course, this is only a guess, but most experts seem to feel that few technological breakthroughs will be made during this period and that the coming decades will not be an era of product innovation. Newspapers may claim that nuclear fusion, biotechnology, and superconductivity will lead to product innovations, but judging from current technological trends, it will not be quite that simple. In the case of television and computers, for example, it took nearly a hundred years before these technologies could be commercialized and enter our lives. Despite successes in the laboratory, it is premature to think that nuclear fusion and superconductors will soon have much impact on manufacturing or the economy or everyday living.

In thinking about U.S.–Japan relations from the perspective of technology, the structure of the frictions in this area becomes clearer if we make a distinction between product innovation and process innovation. Simply put, the cause of the frictions can be traced to the methods Japan has traditionally adopted: Japanese corporations have taken the product innovations developed in the United States, made radical improvements to them, and then exported the finished products back to America. America's dissatisfactions arise from the fact that, even though the United States has heavily financed basic research and new product development, Japan has always been the one to reap the rewards. This has been true in the case of cars, television, and transistor radios, and Americans are consequently fearful that if they let Japan in the door, it will steal the entire house.

From a historical perspective, however, the basic research and development stage of technology has usually occurred in one country and the application and improvement stage somewhere else. All technologies have taken this route before being disseminated worldwide. Thus, although one can sympathize with America's feelings of disappointment, one cannot fault Japan and claim that it has been underhanded. On the contrary, by improving the technology it has received, Japanese process innovation has made a significant contribution to the world and to the human race.

When it comes to the question of who wins and who loses, however, America is clearly the loser and Japan is clearly the winner. This has been a cause for American anger and has contributed to the deterioration of U.S.–Japan relations. The fact is that huge amounts of money are needed for basic research and the development of product innovations. These are also very risky areas where the prospects of success may be virtually nonexistent. But someone has to do basic research and develop new products, for without product innovation there would be no process innovation.

What made the product innovation of the 1950s and 1960s possible was World War II. Patents and innovative technologies that Germany had possessed flowed into America, Britain, and Russia along with Jewish scientists fleeing Nazi persecution, not to mention the German scientists who emigrated after the war. We should not forget that nuclear energy, chemical products, and new materials such as plastics were all technologies developed for military use. In fact, without a war, it is very difficult to develop truly innovative technologies. At least, that has been the case historically.

Seen in this light, the view of some experts that the 1990s and the early twenty-first century will be a dark age for technology may well be correct. As long as the world continues to be relatively peaceful, the technological mainstream will be process innovation, that is, the gradual improvement of technologies that already exist. Thus, we perhaps should not expect too much in the way of product innovations on the magnitude of computers, communications technology, and nuclear energy that have radically changed our lives.

If, however, in the years leading up to the twenty-first century breakthroughs are made in space technology and the other areas of basic research in which the United States has been investing vast sums of money for the past forty years, then we may see a period of product innovation centered in America like that of the fifties and sixties. Needless to say, this would be desirable not only for the United States but for Japan and the rest of the world. If a new wave of product innovation does not come out of America and the present trend of process innovation based on existing technologies continues, then inevitably all eyes will turn to Japan, which has had outstanding success in this area. If that happens, Japan may very well find that the anger and irritation of America and the criticisms of the rest of the world will grow even stronger.

Fostering Basic Research. There are many kinds of technology—technology for popular consumption, such as the consumer electronics in which Japan prides itself, and large-scale space and military technology like the NASA space shuttle. As Shintaro Ishihara takes pride in pointing out, Japanese silicon chips are enormously superior to those of any other country, but microchips are not all there is to technology. As for his argument that Japan could have changed the balance of power by withholding its chips from the United States and selling them to the Soviet Union, it completely misses the broader issues. If Ishihara is trying to say that the Japanese should have more confidence and pride in their country's technology, then he has a point, but statements like his have provoked anti-Japanese feelings among the American people and have caused great damage to U.S.–Japan relations.

Cutting off the supply of Japanese microchips to the United States would certainly cause a temporary dislocation, but it would hardly be a fatal blow. As I mentioned earlier, America has any number of ways it could retaliate. It could cut off supplies of oil, natural resources, and food to Japan as it did to the former Soviet Union under the provisions of COCOM during the cold war. It could also cut off the flow of technology. Ironically, as Akio Morita of Sony said, if worse came to worst, the United States could get along without Japan, but Japan could not get along without the United States. That is no reason, however, to downgrade Japanese technology. Considering how far Japan has gotten after starting out from nothing slightly more than forty-five years ago, we Japanese should feel very proud and give credit where credit is due. But we must also not forget the fact that much of our success is due to friendly relations between Japan and the United States.

Because Japanese process innovation has been so successful, Japan has been the target of the half-envious criticism that the Japanese people are copycats who lack creativity. Are the Japanese people somehow naturally unsuited for product innovation? As history makes clear, that is not at all the case. In the Edo period (1600-1868), Japanese developed a type of electricity and the *wadokei,* a clock unlike any developed elsewhere in the world. Although the length of night and day varies with the seasons, the wadokei was devised to read the same time each day at sunrise and at sundown. It did so by adjusting the length of the units of time depending on the season of the year. In winter, for example, when the nights are long, an hour would be considerably longer than an hour in the daytime when the period between sunrise and sunset is short. Conversely, in the summertime an hour during the day would be longer than an hour at night. The concept and the technology that went into producing the wadokei are true examples of Japanese originality.

Since the war, however, the Japanese have had no need to demonstrate this sort of originality. Japanese companies have been able to produce a steady stream of new products simply by making improvements to American product innovations. Moreover, these goods have met with enormous commercial success. That in itself is no cause for criticism nor should its importance be downplayed. If France or Britain had thought to do what Japan was doing, they too could have made use of American technology. But they did not do so. Japan deserves to be given credit for what it has been able to accomplish.

But skill in process innovation will not be sufficient in the future. If Japan wants the rest of the world to stop calling it a copycat, let alone acknowledge it as a technological superpower, it must pour at least as much money and effort into basic research and product innovation as it currently spends on process innovation. The government and the private sector must join forces to insure that basic research receives ample financial support as it has in the United States.

The greatest stumbling block to developing product innovation in Japan is its educational system. A standardized system that aims at uniformity cannot foster originality. But the problem is rooted even more deeply in Japanese society itself, where a nail that stands out is beaten down and any expressions of individuality are thwarted. Originality is unlikely to evolve except in a society like America that respects individuality and makes allowances for lone wolves and eccentrics. This tolerance and acceptance encourage the exceptionally talented to excel in their areas of expertise instead of alienating them for their uniqueness. What is needed is a loose and flexible social framework that can give geniuses and remarkable talents the room they need to flourish.

I was quite impressed by what I saw several years ago when I dropped in on Professor Marvin Minsky's laboratory at MIT. Professor Minsky is the number-one authority on artificial intelligence in America. His students are unconventional, to say the least. One was taking a nap in the lobby in front of the lab, holding a computer in his lap; another was sitting cross-legged and meditating. At first glance it did not seem like a lab at all. When Professor Minsky called for his assistant, the latter was nowhere to be found. A friend appeared and said that the assistant had gone out to lunch and had not yet come back. It was well after four o'clock, but Minsky seemed quite unperturbed. The whole group, in fact, was a bit odd. In Japan such people would be treated at best as eccentric, at worst as crazy. But America is a society that tolerates unconventional behavior and respects originality. At IBM ordinary employees wear suits and ties, but those who work in the laboratory are allowed to wear whatever they want and come and go as they please. Only from such freedom can originality arise.

Japan, in contrast, is a strongly group-oriented society that does not tolerate displays of individuality. As I've already discussed, being late is not allowed. Moreover, employees who do not faithfully follow the rules laid down by their company regarding morning exercises or calisthenics are ostracized.

When my children were of school age, every spring they went to school in Japan, and in the fall they came back to the United States and attended school here. They thus experienced the compulsory education systems of both countries. As they grew older, they complained about how much they disliked the group competition in Japanese schools, one of the more stifling aspects of standardized education. In Japanese schools children are divided into groups, and every opportunity is seized to encourage group competition. What my children found most difficult were tests in *kanji,* the Chinese characters used in the Japanese writing system. Because of their double life, they could not keep up with their Japanese classmates in areas like writing kanji that require constant repetition. For that reason, the groups my children belonged to always lost. The other students began to boycott them and exclude them from their groups.

The worst part of the situation was that the losing group had to kneel on the floor for thirty minutes or spend fifteen minutes filling buckets with water using only their hands. Because this physical punishment was inflicted on the entire group, my children felt humiliated beyond endurance. "We could have taken it if we were the only ones punished," they later told me, "but it is really an absurd system to make other people suffer because of our mistakes."

Compulsory education in Japan is, I imagine, much the same today as it was then. To hope for originality from such a system is impossible. It may be all right for process innovation, but it is certainly not suited for product innovation.

National Emergencies Strengthen Japan. It has been commonly acknowledged that each time Japan has faced a national emergency over the past several decades it has emerged the stronger for it and has used the experience as a springboard for rapid growth. This was true, as we have already seen, with the upward revaluation of the yen in the 1980s, but the most striking example was Japan's response to the oil shocks of the 1970s.

Japan emerged from the two oil shocks as a major world power both economically and technologically. The international balance of payments clearly reveal this fact. At the time of the first oil shock in 1973, Japan's international balance of payments plummeted. Three years later, however, Japan had moved back into the black. The same was true of the second oil shock in 1979: Japan's balance of payments returned to the black within two years, and this surplus position has continued practically unchecked ever since. How were the Japanese able to survive the oil shocks so successfully? First of all, theirs was a triumph of energy-reduction technology. Before the oil shocks, Japan earmarked 3 to 4 percent of its GNP to pay for oil imports; in 1991 the figure was only 0.9 percent. In short, Japan took advantage of the opportunities provided by the oil shocks to become a technological and economic superpower.

On the other hand, no one even by way of flattery could claim that America came through the oil shocks successfully. In some ways, it might even be said that the United States has still not completely recovered from the experience. Many Americans still operate as if gas and oil will always be in cheap supply. When Ross Perot proposed a surtax on gasoline during the 1992 presidential election campaign, the American public was outraged. Despite the fact that the price of gas in the United States is approximately one quarter of the price in Japan, many Americans refuse to recognize or admit that gasoline is a nonreplenishable resource that must be rationed as such. Today the United States, which accounts for 5 percent of the world's population, consumes 25 percent of the total global energy output.

Unlike Japan, where most homes still use space heaters in each room and relatively few houses are centrally heated, in most parts of the United States every house has a central heating unit that uses up enormous amounts of heating fuel. Such extravagant use of oil is not necessarily a bad practice, however. This is related to a concept in economics called "the minimum cost principle," which says that the best plan is to use large quantities of whatever is cheapest. Thus, if oil is the cheapest form of energy, it is proper to use it. But once the propensity to use great quantities of oil has been established, it is hard to respond if the price goes up or the supply is suddenly cut. The American public's very first reaction to the oil shock in the 1970s was that it was a trick by the oil companies. Once they realized it was no trick, they began to demand that the government do something.

I vividly remember the televised appeal to conserve energy that President Nixon made during the winter of the first oil crisis. He asked Americans to lower the temperature inside their homes by a mere three or four degrees and to maintain an economical speed when driving. But the Oval Room of the White House, from which he was speaking, was obviously comfortably heated, and those who watched him were more than likely sitting in their shirtsleeves in equally warm rooms. Until then most Americans had never tried to conserve oil.

At one time during the oil shock, kerosene stoves

were popular among Americans who wanted to cut down on their oil bills. Due to differences in state laws, however, they cannot be used everywhere. At that time I was living in Rhode Island, where their use was legal, so when I learned that kerosene stoves were being sold at a department store in neighboring Massachusetts, I decided to buy one. "If you buy this space heater," the salesclerk told me, "you can't use it in Massachusetts." The stove was being sold in Massachusetts, but it could not be used there because state law forbids the indoor use of any appliance that emits a flame on the grounds that this poses a fire hazard. Even if many Americans had been willing to conserve energy by using kerosene stoves, state laws prevented them from doing so. Thus, no matter how earnestly the President may appeal for cooperation, it is not as easy for Americans to fall into line as it is for the Japanese.

Although slow to respond, some three or four years after the first oil shock the U.S. government finally launched an energy-conservation policy. Under the energy credit system, money spent to conserve energy was tax deductible. For example, if a home owner spent $4,000 to install insulation, replace windows and doors, and make other home improvements to keep out the cold, that amount could be deducted from his or her income tax. An appeal to the pocketbook will stir even Americans into action. So an energy-reduction program at last got under way.

Japan responded to the oil shocks in the 1970s in several ways. The Japanese public immediately cut back on spending and started saving a larger proportion of their disposable income. To counter this decrease in domestic consumption Japan launched an "export drive" to raise enough funds to pay for the higher oil prices. The Japanese labor force was willing to work harder, and this boost in productivity compensated for the decreased use of energy. The Japanese government then stepped in by increasing public investment expenditures for energy-saving capital formation and infrastructure investment. Energy-saving technology was developed such as a new generation of quiet, energy-efficient air conditioning units that can be used to both heat and cool a room.

America was not just slow in investing in energy-conservation technology, both the government and the private sector utterly ignored the need for such technology. This was because America is a people-centered society that prefers to spend money on policies that will keep the public happy rather than on technologies to conserve energy. In this regard, too, the responses in the United States and Japan were completely different.

The differences between the two countries' responses to the oil shocks are very great. When faced with this unprecedented national emergency, Japanese corporations froze wage increases, and even the labor unions went along with the decision. In America, however, when energy costs went up because of the oil shock, labor unions demanded pay raises on the grounds that rising costs had made life more difficult. Japanese companies used the crisis to strengthen themselves, but U.S. companies were weakened by it. If we factor in the development of energy-conservation technology, then it is obvious why Japan rapidly became a creditor superpower in the 1980s while America slumped to the status of the world's biggest debtor nation.

Can Japan Avoid
International Isolation?

The Folly of Voluntary Restraint. As an economist I am
an advocate of free trade, but I do not believe that trade
is everything. Top priority must be given to a country's
overall prosperity and its continued survival. Considered from this perspective, Japan must avoid alienating
itself from the international community by incurring
resentment for behavior that is considered undesirable
or unacceptable to the community at large. To prevent
international isolation, Japan will probably have to
change its ways, and this may entail a fair amount of
pain. Circumstances may even arise that will require
some sacrifices in the area of trade. The foremost concern is repairing and stabilizing U.S.–Japan relations.
Ways must be found that will take a form acceptable to
both the United States and Japan and that will not leave
Japan isolated.

America's ideas on the subject are quite clear. The
United States wants to maintain a system that allows it
to buy whatever it wants without any restraints whatsoever and to sell freely whatever it wants to sell; to
achieve a trade balance; and to preserve its superpower status. The long history of U.S.–Japan trade disputes has always been one of conflict over how to
achieve a bilateral balance of trade. The Structural Impediments Initiative talks in 1989–90 took the form
they did because America had learned its lesson from
its long-standing disputes with Japan.

Take, for instance, the dispute over automobiles.
During the late 1970s and early 1980s frictions arose

between the two countries over car imports. The decision in 1981 that Japan should adopt a policy of "voluntary restraint" on automobile exports was the worst possible option for the United States not only because it was contrary to the American policy of free trade, but because the situation demanded policies to strengthen an industry that had grown weak. Instead, the United States chose a policy of balanced contraction that progressively weakened the industry even further. As a result of cuts in supply, the price of Japanese cars skyrocketed, and Japanese carmakers pocketed the windfall.

If a particular company or industry seems on the verge of collapse, what options are possible? From the economist's point of view, the correct answer in the long run is to jettison that company or industry. But such a policy would not be politically expedient, so the short-term alternative is to have the government step in to save it. In the case of the auto industry, the best policy in the short term would have been to give financial aid and preferential tax treatment to Chrysler. But, if for some reason that was impossible, the second-best policy would have been to save the auto industry as a whole. Since that would have cost too much, the third-best method would have been to protect the American auto industry by slapping tariffs on cars entering from Japan. The worst possible choice was to have Japanese carmakers voluntarily agree to limit the number of cars they exported.

From the perspective of economics, these are the four available options in descending order of desirability. But from the political perspective the order is just the reverse. To the economist, a Chrysler bailout is the best and least expensive policy, but given the nature of American society, choosing that option would raise serious problems politically. American public opinion would not tolerate the government's use of tax money on behalf of a particular commercial enterprise.

Japanese find this all very puzzling. If a company in the private sector is in a bit of a slump, what is wrong with using American taxpayers' money to bail it out? The answer to this question is simple. If President Reagan had ignored the American people's antipathy to the idea of a bailout, he would not have been re-elected. The second-best policy, saving the entire auto-motive industry, was also unacceptable to the American public because of the huge expense that this would entail. The third-best option was raising tariffs, but Reagan, being by nature a free trader, resisted abandoning his own policies and placing tariffs on Japanese cars. Free trade, which has been U.S. policy since the end of the war, has come to symbolize the very essence of the American way. Reagan could not disown it, so that option too was out.

That left only what economists would consider the worst possible choice—voluntary restrictions on exports. The actual phrase used, "voluntary restraint," sounded quite good. After all, if Japan wanted to limit its automobile exports of its own free will, there was nothing more to be said. Politically, it was the most expedient option, and Reagan, of course, jumped at it. But in the final analysis voluntary restraint was a restriction on free trade, nonetheless. And it has had the worst possible consequences for the United States. First, as supply contracted, car prices doubled. This price rise breathed new life into Chrysler and the other

American carmakers, but consumers found themselves having to pay high prices for cars. Secondly, when prices rose and American carmakers began to make money again, they did not bother to capitalize on the situation. Instead of laying plans to increase their competitiveness while the supply of Japanese cars was limited, they were content to sit back and relax.

Japan's voluntary restraint on exports, therefore, had no beneficial results whatsoever. Americans soon learned that encouraging voluntary restraint was a form of economic suicide. For that reason, during the last round of trade talks, the U.S. side shifted gears and began to say to Japan, "we will not put restrictions on Japan's exports, so don't put any restrictions on American exports." In short, Japan has to open its markets.

When the dispute over automobiles arose, Japan ought to have said "no" to voluntary restraints. It should have explained all the disadvantages and pointed out that adopting such a policy would further undermine American competitiveness. Thanks to Japan's obliging "yes," efforts to solve the underlying problems were postponed, and the result was a further deterioration in U.S.–Japanese relations. What makes the situation even worse is that Japanese carmakers profited from the voluntary restraint agreement because they could sell their allotted quota practically without any effort. Negligible marketing costs, coupled with the low yen/high dollar exchange rate current at the time, meant that Japanese carmakers could just sit back and rake in the profits.

Voluntary restraints also meant the creation of an export cartel. Toyota, Nissan, and Honda were able to export a predetermined number of cars without competing with one another. But instead of relaxing their efforts they decided to make even more money by shifting to the high end of the line, that is, from cars for the masses to luxury automobiles. This decision meant even greater losses for the U.S. car industry.

America now realizes this and has decided to fight Japanese exports with American exports. It may not be able to win with cars, but there are other areas where American competitiveness is still strong. Threatening to invoke the Super 301 clause while launching an export offensive in the areas of satellites, supercomputers, and lumber is probably a natural turn of events.

Now Is the Time to Create a Japan with a Human Face. Since the mid to late 1980s the key word in Japan has been *kokusaika* (internationalization). But though the word is on everyone's lips, Japan's internationalization has hitherto been directed exclusively outward, and few people in Japan seem to have reflected on the frictions this has caused. I recall reading a *New York Times* article about five years ago which made the scathing comment that the internationalization the Japanese talk so much about is nothing more than young people eating Italian pasta on the Ginza, dating *gaijin* (foreigners), and paying high prices to see Michael Jackson and Madonna live; worst of all, they buy condominiums in Manhattan and think this is internationalization—an observation not far off the mark.

Japan is becoming more and more isolated. If this trend is to be reversed, the *kokusaika* that Japan must now aspire to is the second stage in the process: a true internationalization from within. Just as Japanese goods, money, and people have hitherto flowed freely overseas, Japan will now have to accept the influx of goods, money, and people from abroad. If an internal internationalization can be fully realized, Japan-bashing, U.S.–Japan trade disputes, and the Japan-is-different argument will all evaporate.

Allowing Japanese companies to go on buying American companies, but not allowing Japanese companies to be sold to Americans—by virtue of the fact that institutional investors, especially cross-shareholders, are unwilling to sell their holdings at any price—is in the same spirit as Japan's refusal to import a single grain of rice. As Japan proceeds with the second half of its internationalization process, it must remember that as long as its economic logic does not correspond with that of the rest of the world, international isolation will be unavoidable.

One extreme scenario for the future is that trade frictions will continue until Japan becomes America's fifty-first state. This may be a gross exaggeration, but if Japan accedes to all of America's demands, that is in essence what will happen. Making the flow of people, money, and goods between the United States and Japan absolutely free and imposing exactly the same social and economic rules on both countries would amount to just that. Under those circumstances, what would happen to Japan's culture and traditions? Would Silicon Valleys spring up in the rice-producing districts of Akita and Niigata? Would the rice fields become overgrown with weeds and the festivals in which villagers pray for a good harvest be replaced with high-tech inspired holidays? Perhaps so. That would certainly put an end to U.S.–Japan disputes and prevent Japan from becoming isolated internationally.

But whether such changes would be a good thing, whether they would make the Japanese people happy, is a different question. A country that does not have its own culture and traditions cannot survive. What, then, is to be done? I believe Japanese should comply firmly and willingly if not to America's demands, then to the intentions that underlie them.

Japan-bashing in America is inevitable because the United States has two serious dissatisfactions with Japan. The first is its trade deficit with Japan that runs close to $50 billion a year. The second is the over-presence of "Japan money" that in the late 1980s flooded into the country buying up American companies and real estate. The United States would like to make these two complaints disappear by fighting Japanese exports with U.S. exports and by countering "buying America" with "buying Japan." If this happens, if the two countries achieve a bilateral trade balance and parity in their direct investment activities, disputes between the United States and Japan would spontaneously disappear. These goals should not be too difficult to achieve.

For example, Japan's trade surplus with the United States is now close to $50 billion a year, roughly three-quarters of which, some $37.5 billion, comes from car sales alone. If car exports stopped, the American trade deficit would immediately shrink to one-quarter of its present size. The impact would be enormous. Japanese carmakers would be furious, of course, but Japan has gone on exporting manufactured goods for too long, and the Japanese industrial world has made too much conspicuous profit from automobiles. It seems a small price to pay compared with exchanging Japan's traditional culture for "high-tech inspired holidays."

In other words, if Japan is not willing to submit tamely to becoming America's fifty-first state, it must sharply reduce its exports to the United States and sharply increase its imports. Then, when a trade balance is achieved, if Japanese want to buy property in America, Japan should recognize the right of Americans to buy an equivalent amount in Japan. A relationship in which one neighbor is free to go into another's yard and rearrange the shrubbery and paving stones, but tells his neighbor to "stay out of my yard" can no longer be sanctioned. Moreover, Japan should start moving in a more consumer-oriented direction. It needs to raise its standard of living to Western levels and give the Japanese people an "affluence dividend" so they do not have to save so much. It needs to reform its money games such as land speculation and its money politics—the political scandals over influence peddling such as the Recruit affair and more recently the Sagawa Kyubin incident—that have given the country such a bad image abroad. And finally it needs to put a stop to the self-aggrandizement of those mysterious legal entities that call themselves corporations.

Although not the "Amerippon" concept that Brzezinski proposed, such moves would gradually help to create a human face for Japan that would facilitate cooperation with the United States. It certainly would help keep Japan from international isolation. But as long as the Japanese people identify themselves more closely with the corporations they work for than with their

country as a whole; as long as they regard the corporation and not the state as the ultimate source of their
"life, liberty, and the pursuit of happiness," then the
corporations will continue to speak for Japan, the Japanese people will remain disassociated from international politics, and Japan will find itself increasingly
isolated from the rest of the world.

Japan in the World: Global You-ism. Not only must Japan take up the domestic task of enacting internal reforms, it must also meet the challenge of dealing with
global issues. Japan has long been a silent, faceless
nation in international affairs. Few Japanese are either
willing or able to speak to the world. Whenever a major
crisis arises, there is a great deal of irresponsible, unrealistic discussion in Japan but few substantive proposals of how Japan might become involved in a solution.
Usually the government comes up with the funds to
make up for its paucity of effort and imagination. No
wonder people regard Japan as a country that deals
with diplomatic issues with high-sounding words and
checkbook in hand. Japan must reverse the main cause
for its negative image, its parochialism. Today the
"group" upon which the happiness of the Japanese
people ultimately depends is a far cry from the village
of old or the corporation of yesterday; it is the world
community—all the countries on the face of the globe.

In the field of economics, Japanese-style capitalism,
the so-called "Japanese model," is frequently cited as
an example of unprecedented economic success. The
Japanese economy, however, is now being forced to
make major policy changes and will have to make a
gradual shift away from the Japanese model to a more

mature Western style of capitalism. If that is the case, will the Japanese model that has won such acclaim simply vanish into thin air? Is it nothing more than an idle flowering that can only bloom in the soil of a country others regard as "different" and "unfair"? I do not think so.

The Japanese model should function quite effectively in South American countries like Brazil and Argentina, for example, that cannot seem to escape from their enormous international debt. Or in Eastern European countries like Hungary, Czechoslovakia, and Poland that have renounced communism and rushed headlong into free trade but have yet to discover ways to rebuild their economies. Of course, it could also be introduced and applied in the five dragons—Korea, Taiwan, Singapore, Hong Kong, and Thailand: then, in Indonesia and the Philippines; and perhaps in the future even in China. In fact, it is probably reasonable to believe that the model would work even more effectively in these Asian countries because their values and ways of thinking are similar to Japan's. But if Japan does try to introduce the principles of Japanese-style management into Asia, it must proceed cautiously and with the full understanding and cooperation of these countries so that it does not repeat the mistakes of the old Greater East Asia Co-prosperity Sphere.

Even if the present Japanese model can continue to live on in other countries, in what direction should the Japanese economy itself proceed? To put it bluntly, Japan has gotten too much of a free ride from the international system. Although it has become a major economic power, it has also acquired an image in international society as an egocentric country that is only concerned with its own interests. If Japan is to win world approval, it must shed its parochial image and start showing a spirit of altruism. In contrast to the traditional group-mindedness of Japan—its "we-ism"—it must develop a new spirit of "global you-ism."

The first key area in a program of global you-ism is the environment. Japan should play a leading role in efforts to protect against, control, and reverse environmental damage. By contributing money and manpower to environmental problems, Japan would emerge as the guardian of our planet. If it does not play a role of this magnitude, it will not be able to reverse its unfavorable image. There are five major problems facing the global environment: global warming, acid rain, the thinning of the ozone layer, the disappearance of the rain forests and the ecological disruption this is causing, and the pollution of the oceans. What makes matters most difficult is that these five problems are intricately interrelated. If Japan could meet the enormous challenge of solving these problems, or at least make serious efforts to do so, the world's image of Japan would change from negative to positive.

The second key area is hunger. It is unconscionable in this day and age that so many people still die of hunger worldwide. Now is the time for Japan to develop a foreign aid policy that treats rice as an international public good. To be more precise, Japan should buy large quantities of foreign rice and ship it directly from the United States or elsewhere to countries where people are starving, thereby circumventing the Staple Food Control Act that forbids rice imports to Japan. By so doing Japan would be able to respond to criticism on two counts: its efforts to open its markets and its contributions to international society. Japan is now a major provider of official development assistance. But Japan's financial aid in this area is actually used by recipient nations to buy plant, technology, and products from Japan. The beneficiaries of Japan's ODA policies have been Japanese trading houses and manufacturers. However, it is now time to review Japan's agricultural policy with two objectives in mind: first, permitting the purchase of rice from Thailand, the United States, and other countries to be used abroad for humanitarian purposes; and, second, using ODA to assist the domestic agricultural sector by moving away from the current system of paying farmers not to grow rice and instead allowing them to produce as much rice as they want and using any surplus as part of Japan's overseas aid program. This would indeed be a plus-sum solution that would please the United States and other rice-exporting countries and help Japanese farmers increase their productivity.

The third key area is basic research. After the war, the Japanese government and Japanese corporations sent large numbers of their most talented engineers and researchers to study in the labs at MIT and other American universities. Japan was able to do this because America willingly accepted foreign students. In Japan, however, most research is done not in universities but in the laboratories of Japan's leading corporations, which are reluctant to open their doors to receive the world's students and researchers or to share research information on the grounds that such information constitutes trade secrets. Such a one-way street will not be tolerated much longer. Japan will have to make up for the research-related losses that America has suffered. It will have to be magnanimous and give the world a "free ride" on Japanese research.

Unless Japan is isolated internationally and shut out of the international marketplace, it will probably go on making money and running up surpluses. The future of Japan will be determined by how it uses those surpluses. Japan's egocentric attitudes must change as the world grows smaller and all countries share the same fate.

SELECTED
BIBLIOGRAPHY

Brzezinski, Zbigniew K. *The Grand Failure: The Birth and Death of Communism in the Twentieth Century.* New York: Scribner, 1989.

Fallows, James. "Containing Japan." *Atlantic Monthly,* May 1989.

Flath, D. "Why Are There So Many Retail Stores in Japan?" *Japan and the World Economy* 2 (1990):365–86.

Ishihara, Shintaro. *The Japan That Can Say "No."* New York: Simon & Schuster, 1992.

Ito, T., and M. Maruyama. "Is the Japanese Distribution System Really Inefficient?" In *Trade with Japan,* edited by P. Krugman. Chicago: University of Chicago Press, 1992.

Johnson, Chalmers A. *MITI and the Japanese Miracle: The Growth of Industrial Policy, 1925–1975.* Stanford: Stanford University Press, 1982.

Kennedy, Paul. *Grand Strategies in War and Peace.* New Haven: Yale University Press, 1991.

Komiya, R., M. Okuno, and K. Suzumura, eds. *Industrial Policy in Japan.* Tokyo: University of Tokyo Press, 1984. (In Japanese).

Kuribayashi, S. "Present Situation and Future Prospects of Japan's Distribution System." *Japan and the World Economy* 3 (1991):39–60.

Miwa, Yoshiro, and Kiyohiko G. Nishimura. *The Distribution System in Japan.* Tokyo: University of Tokyo Press, 1991. (In Japanese).

Montgomery, David B. "Understanding the Japanese as Customers, Competitors, and Collaborators." *Japan and the World Economy* 3 (1991):61–91.

Morita, Akio, and Shintaro Ishihara. *The Japan That Can Say "No."* 1989. Tokyo: Kobunsha, 1991. (In Japanese).

Morita, Akio, Edwin M. Reingold, and Mitsuko Shimonura. *Made in Japan: Akio Morita and Sony.* New York: E. P. Dutton, 1986.

Sato, Ryuzo, Rama Ramachandran, and Elias C. Grivoyannis. "National Economic Policies in Japan." In *National Economic Policies: Handbook of Comparative Economic Policies,* vol. 1, edited by Dominick Salvatore. New York: Greenwood Press, 1991.

Sato, R., and G. Suzawa. *Research and Productivity: Endogenous Technical Change.* Boston: Auburn House, 1983.

INDEX

211

Richardson, Elliot, 7
*Rise and Fall of the Great Powers,
The* (Kennedy)
  basic assumptions of, 142–44
  Japan and, 138–39
  refutation of, 139
R. J. Reynolds Industries, merger
  with, 156
R.J.R. Nabisco, LBO by, 156
Rockefeller, Nelson, viii
Rockefeller Center, selling of, 5, 16,
  117, 124, 131, 133, 135
Rules, unwritten, 75, 80–83
Russia
  democratization in, xii
  free-market economy in, 21
  See also Soviet Union

"Salad bowl" society, 162
  values of, 98–102
Samuelson, Paul, 147, 151
  law of economic conservation
    and, 179
Sanctions, 149
  imposing, 14
Sato, Eisaku, 45
*Scale and Scope: The Dynamics of
Industrial Capitalism* (Chandler),
  40
Scandals, 142, 175–76
Schlumberger, 43
Security. *See* National security
Security treaty, U.S.–Japan, 62–63,
  64
Segment pricing, 120
Self-denial, 89–90, 91–92
Semiconductor market, foreign
  share of, 55
Seniority system, 150
Sensationalism, media and, 15–16,
  93, 132
Shimura, Fumio, 10
Shinkansen Bullet train, 152
Shopping, Japanese and, 122, 123

SII talks. *See* Structural Impedi-
  ments Initiative talks
Small outlets
  decline of, 123–24
  high density of, 122, 123
Smith, Adam, 59
Social goods. *See* Public goods
Social progress, 83, 108
Social Security, national deficit and,
  101–2
Sole agency dealership system,
  120
Sony, 58, 160
  Columbia Pictures and, 16
"Sources of Soviet Conduct, The"
  (Kennan), 3–4
Soviet Union
  collapse of, xiv, 3, 21
  See also Russia
Space heaters, 193
  energy saving with, 194
Space technology, 186
Stable stockholders, 157, 158
Standardized education, 190–91
Staple Food Control Act (1942), 50,
  115, 116, 206
Stereotypes, xiv, 91
  dealing with, 73–94
Stevenson, Adlai, viii
Stock economy, 167, 168
Stockholders
  consideration for, 160
  stable, 157, 158
Stock market system, 156
Stock prices, increase in, 159–61
Stock superpower, Japan as, 168
Structural differences, 18, 19
Structural Impediments Initiative
  (SII) talks, 13–14, 18, 19, 25, 32,
  34, 50, 70, 120, 121, 123, 155, 161,
  167, 196
Subcontractors, 149–55, 158
Summers, Lawrence, 62
  on *The Japan That Can Say
    "No,"* 56–57